Ancient Peoples and Places

THE
GEORGIANS

General Editor

DR. GLYN DANIEL

ABOUT THE AUTHOR

David Marshall Lang studied at St John's College, Cambridge, where he was a Major Scholar and later held a Fellowship. Military and official duties took him to Persia during the Second World War. In 1949 he joined the staff of the School of Oriental and African Studies, University of London, first as Lecturer in Georgian, then as Reader and, from 1964, Professor of Caucasian Studies. During the year 1952–53, he held a Senior Fellowship at the Russian Institute of Columbia University, New York, and in 1964–65 was visiting Professor of Caucasian Languages at the University of California, Los Angeles. From 1962 until 1964 he was Honorary Secretary of the Royal Asiatic Society, London.

Professor Lang is the author of a number of other volumes on Georgian and Russian themes, the principal of these being Lives and Legends of the Georgian Saints (1956), The First Russian Radical (1959) *and* A Modern History of Georgia (1962).

Ancient Peoples and Places

THE
GEORGIANS

David Marshall Lang

74 PHOTOGRAPHS
45 LINE DRAWINGS
4 MAPS
I TABLE

FREDERICK A. PRAEGER
Publishers
New York · Washington

THIS IS VOLUME FIFTY-ONE IN THE SERIES

Ancient Peoples and Places

GENERAL EDITOR: DR. GLYN DANIEL

BOOKS THAT MATTER

*Published in the United States of America
in 1966 by Frederick A. Praeger, Inc.,
Publishers, 111 Fourth Avenue,
New York 3, N.Y.*
*© David Marshall Lang 1966
Library of Congress Catalog Card Number: 66-19951
Printed in Great Britain*

CONTENTS

LIST OF ILLUSTRATIONS   7

FOREWORD   12

CHRONOLOGICAL TABLE   14

I   GENERAL CHARACTERISTICS AND EARLY ORIGINS   17

II   COPPER AND BRONZE   36

III   TRIBES, MYTHS AND TRAVELLER'S TALES   54

IV   CAUCASIAN IBERIA AND COLCHIS IN CLASSICAL TIMES   72

V   THE GEORGIAN FEUDAL MONARCHY   91

VI   EARLY MEDIEVAL ARCHITEC-TURE AND THE ARTS   119

VII   LITERATURE AND LEARNING   152

BIBLIOGRAPHY   179

SOURCES OF ILLUSTRATIONS 190

THE PLATES 193

NOTES ON THE PLATES 225

INDEX 236

ILLUSTRATIONS

PLATES   1   General view of Mestia

2   Castle and village of Khertvisi

3   The Carnival of *Qeenoba*

4   Collective vineyard in Kakheti

5   Peasant farmer in Imereti

6   Bronze axeheads

7   Necklace from Trialeti

8   Jason taming the Bulls of Aeëtes

9   Gold goblet from Trialeti

10   Gold ferrule from Trialeti

11   Chased silver goblet from Trialeti

12   Bronze engraved axehead

13   Late Bronze Age battle-axe

14   Black burnished clay *pithos*, from Trialeti

15   Stag-shaped bronze standard-head

16   Bronze model horseman

17   Ithyphallic bronze figure

18   Bronze girdle

19   Bronze belt buckle

20   Bronze belt buckle

21   Bronze standard terminal

22   Bronze standard terminal

PLATES 23 Silver sheathed leg of funerary couch,
Bagineti Sarcophagus

24 Cameo pendant and chain

25 Gold necklace and locket

26 Oval garnet intaglio

27 Gold necklace and locket

28 Pair of gold earrings

29 Epitaph of Princess Serapita

30 Roman-style mausoleum

31 General view of Uplistsikhe cave city

32 Interior of a chamber in Uplistsikhe

33 Wall inscription, Bolnisi Sioni church

34 Bolnisi Sioni, general view

35 Interior brick vaulting, Bolnisi Sioni

36 Elevation of the Cross, Jvari church

37 Old Shuamta

38 South façade of Jvari church

39 Church of All Saints

40 Basilica at Dmanisi

41 Kumurdo church

42 Patriarchal cathedral of Sveti-tskhoveli

43 Cathedral of Allaverdi

44 Cathedral of Samtavisi

45 Ruins of the Bagrat Cathedral

46 Pair of fantastic birds, church of Nikordsminda

47 Part of eastern façade, church of Nikordsminda

48 East window of Savane church

8

PLATES 49 Decorated windows, Samtavro church

50 Sculptured capital, Oshki church

51 Sculptured interlace work, Kvatakhevi church

52 View of the monastery at Gelati

53 Ruins of medieval Academy and University of Iqalto

54 Tower of the monastery of Ubisi

55 View of cave monastery of Vardzia

56 Interior view of the principal church, Vardzia

57 Ruins of the twelfth-century palace, Geguti

58 Carved wooden door, Chukuli

59 Carved wooden door, Jakhunderi

60 Fresco in the church at Ateni

61 Fresco at Qindsvisi church

62 Triptych from Martvili monastery

63 Cross of King David the Builder

64 Cross from the Ishkhani monastery

65 Two repoussé plaques from the Shemok-medi monastery

66 Silver roundel of St Mamay, Gelati monastery

67 Silver repoussé plaque from Sagolasheni

68 Part of the cover of the Berta Gospels

69 Detail from the Khakhuli icon

70 Detail from the icon of the Laklakidze family

71 Fresco showing Shota Rustaveli

PLATES   72   Miniatures of scenes from 'The Man in the Panther's Skin'

73   Miniature of the signs of the Zodiac. Leo

74   Coins of Colchis, Iberia and Georgia

FIGURES   1   *Characteristic types of Georgian houses, p. 21*

2   *Svanian 'lion' standard, p. 23*

3   *Georgian alphabet, p. 27*

4   *Inventory of Kurgan XVII, Trialeti, p. 45*

5   *Bronze belt showing hunting scene, Trialeti, pp. 46, 47*

6   *Characteristic Bronze Age swords and daggers, p. 47*

7   *Painted vase from Trialeti, p. 48*

8   *Map; Diffusion of early metallurgy, p. 49*

9   *Bronze Age dolmen tomb, p. 51*

10   *Map: Georgia in the ancient world, p. 55*

11–13   *Koban-Colchian bronze axeheads, pp. 61, 62*

14   *Bronze belt from the Chabarukhi hoard, pp. 62, 63*

15   *Abkhazian eight-oared boat, p. 69*

16   *Map: Colchis and Iberia, p. 73*

17   *Evolution of the Georgian plough, p. 79*

18   *Intaglio sardonyx ring bezel, p. 84*

19   *Plans of Roman bath at Armazis-Khevi, p. 87*

20   *Horse standing before a fire-altar, p. 89*

21   *Map: medieval Georgia, pp. 92, 93*

22   *Arms of the Bagratid dynasty, p. 105*

23   *Bowman and quiver, p. 110*

24   *Maces, p. 111*

FIGURES 25 *Sword in scabbard, p. 112*

26 *Georgian hat styles, p. 113*

27 *Monogram of Queen Tamar, p. 114*

28 *Court robes of King Giorgi III, p. 115*

29 *Principles of construction of Georgian houses, p. 120*

30 *Plan and section of a darbazi, p. 121*

31 *Detail of a darbazi, p. 122*

32 *Details of carved wooden beams, p. 123*

33 *Artistic wood carving, p. 124*

34 *Walled city of Ujarma, p. 125*

35 *Wine-press from Vardzia, p. 126*

36 *Triple basilica at Zegani, plan, p. 127*

37 *All Saints' church at Vachnadziani, plan, p. 129*

38 *Ninodsminda cathedral, plan, p. 131*

39 *Allaverdi cathedral, plan, p. 133*

40 *Cathedral of Sveti-tskhoveli, plan, p. 135*

41 *Bird of prey on a glazed pottery bowl, p. 145*

42 *Lion on a glazed pottery bowl, p. 146*

43 *'Sun face' motif from a fragment of glazed pottery, p. 146*

44 *Bowl with line and spiral pattern, p. 147*

45 *Ancient stringed instruments, p. 151*

46 *Inscription of Abba Antoni, p. 154*

47 *Georgian medieval helmet styles, p. 169*

48 *Lady with unicorn, Georgian costume, p. 172*

49 *Georgian noble ladies' costume, p. 177*

Foreword

A LARGE PART OF THIS BOOK was conceived and written in 1964 and 1965, during a pleasant year as Visiting Professor of Caucasian Languages at the Near Eastern Center of the University of California, Los Angeles. To the Director of the Center, Dr Gustav E. von Grunebaum, as well as to the former Chairman of the Department of Near Eastern and African Languages, Dr Wolf Leslau, heartfelt thanks are expressed, especially as they generously enabled me to visit the Universities of Berkeley, Columbia and Yale, also the Oriental Institute at Chicago, to gain advice and information from my American colleagues. I also recall with appreciation many helpful discussions at Los Angeles with Marija Gimbutas, also a contributor to the 'Ancient Peoples and Places' series, Jay D. Frierman, who works on problems of medieval Georgian ceramics, and Jonas Greenfield, now promoted to a Chair at Berkeley.

This book could not have been attempted without the assistance of another group of excellent friends, my colleagues in Soviet Georgia, who have welcomed me on four visits and shown me over almost every major region and many principal monuments and sites of their magnificent land. Particular gratitude I owe to the Vice-President and staff of the Georgian Society for Friendship and Cultural Relations in Tbilisi, especially Mr Nodar Kochlashvili, my constant companion in my travels, as well as to Professor Vakhtang Beridze, Deputy Director of the Institute of the History of Georgian Art, David Kapanadze, Curator of the Coin Cabinet, and Professor Paata Gugushvili, Director of the Institute of Economics and Law. Mr Beridze personally selected the bulk of the photographs from the fine collections of the Georgian State Museum in Tbilisi, and the attractiveness of the illustrations is largely due to his taste and discrimination. The last plate, showing the early history of coinage in Georgia, was prepared from casts made by the technical staff of the Coin Room of the British Museum by kind courtesy of the Keeper, Mr G. K. Jenkins.

Finally, I must express the pleasure I have felt at this occasion to collaborate with the General Editor of the 'Ancient Peoples and Places' series, Dr Glyn Daniel, a fellow Johnian and good friend over a period of twenty years, as well as with the genial and expert staff of Messrs Thames and Hudson, notably Mr Eric Peters, Mr Jean-Claude Peissel and Mr Peter Clayton. Their candid and constructive criticism has saved me from many a blunder.

D.M.L.

CHRONOLOGICAL TABLE

Georgian Neolithic culture	*from* 5000 BC
Chalcolithic (Kuro-Araxes) culture	*circa* 3000–2200
Khirbet Kerak ware in Palestine	*circa* 2600–2400
Georgian Early Bronze Age	*from* 2200
Indo-European immigration into Georgia	*circa* 2100
High point of Trialeti *kurgan* culture	*circa* 1500
Fall of Hittite Empire	1200–1190
Mushki dispersed by Tiglath-pileser I of Assyria	1100
Georgian Late Bronze Age	*circa* 1100–700
King Asia of Daiaeni captured by Salmanesar III of Assyria	845
King Menua of Urartu captures Shashilu	790
Sarduri II of Urartu invades Colchis	750–741
Scythians and Cimmerians invade Georgia	730
Greek colonies in Colchis	*from* 600
Fall of Urartu	590
Xenophon and his Ten Thousand traverse south-western Georgia	400
Formation of Iberian kingdom	*from* 400
Reign of Mithradates Eupator of Pontus	120–63
Pompey's Caucasian campaigns	66–65
	BC
	AD
Vespasian fortifies Mtskheta castle	75
Georgian embassies to Hadrian	117–138
Armazi writing: bilingual tombstone of Serapita	*circa* 150
Conversion of Iberia by Saint Nino	330
Life and ministry of Peter the Iberian	409–488
Reign of King Vakhtang Gorgaslan	446–510
Martyrdom of Saint Shushanik	476

Completion of Bolnisi cathedral	492–93
Armeno-Georgian monophysite synod of Dvin	506
King Tsate of Lazica baptized	523
King Gubaz II of Lazica assassinated by Greeks	553
Duke Stephen I of Iberia issues coins and builds Jvari church at Mtskheta	590–607
Greeks and Khazars capture Tbilisi	627
Arabs occupy Eastern Georgia	655
Caliph's forces ravage Georgia	736–38
Beginning of Georgian national chronology	780
Reign of Ashot the Great, Kuropalates	780–826
Martyrdom of Saint Abo	786
Ministry of Saint Gregory of Khandzta	790–861
Adarnase IV becomes 'King of the Georgians'	888
Life and ministry of Euthymius the Athonite	955–1028
Bagrat III becomes King of Kartli	975
General Tornik the Georgian defeats Bardas Scleros	979
Iviron Monastery founded on Mount Athos	980
Death of David Kuropalates; disputes with Byzantium	1001
Bagrat cathedral completed at Kutaisi	1003
Basil Bulgaroktonos invades Georgia	1021
Cathedral of Life-Giving Pillar at Mtskheta completed by Master Constantine Arsukidze	1029
Seljuk Turks invade Georgia	*from* 1065
Reign of King David the Builder	1089–1125
Synod of Ruisi-Urbnisi	1103
Neo-Platonism introduced into Georgia by Ioane Petritsi	*circa* 1105–25
Building of Gelati monastery and academy	1106–1125
Turks and Saracens routed at Didgori	1121
David the Builder captures Tbilisi from Muslim emirs	1122
Georgians occupy part of Armenia	1123
Birth of national bard Shota Rustaveli (traditional date)	1166
Georgians occupy Derbent, on Caspian Sea	1167
Insurrection of Prince Demna and Ivane Orbeli	1177

King Giorgi III appoints Tamar co-regnant of Georgia	1178
Reign of Queen Tamar	1184–1213
Constitutional movement headed by Kutlu Arslan	1185
Tamar's second marriage, to David Soslan	1189
Battle of Shamkhori	1195
Georgians and Greeks found Empire of Trezibond	1204
Battle of Basiani	1204
Capture of Kars by Georgia	1206
Georgians invade Iran	1208–1210
Reign of Tamar's son, Giorgi Lasha	1213–23
Eastern Georgia overrun and subjugated by Mongols	1236

CHAPTER I

General Characteristics and Early Origins

TODAY ONE OF THE MOST markedly individual peoples of the Soviet Union, the Georgians claim the attention of historians and archaeologists by the richness and variety of their ancient material culture and the continuity of their corporate social organization, the evolution of which can be traced back with confidence over a span of three thousand years, while there is evidence to suggest that peoples of palaeo-Caucasian stock, ancestors of the Georgians of today, occupied their present homeland and adjoining areas for a long period prior to this.

The habitat of the Georgians and closely related Ibero-Caucasian peoples forms a wedge-shaped area at the eastern end of the Black Sea. To the north, it is bounded by the main Caucasus range, to the south by Armenia, and to the east by modern Azerbaijan, the Albania of the classical geographers. By far the greater part of the Georgian nation of today is concentrated within the boundaries of the Georgian Soviet Socialist Republic. Of a world total of some three and a half million persons of Georgian and cognate Ibero-Caucasian stock, it was officially calculated in 1959 that 2,601,000 live within Soviet Georgia, where Georgians make up 64·3 per cent of the total population. Another fifty thousand live in various other parts of the U.S.S.R. and the remainder abroad, with large concentrations in the eastern provinces of Turkey and also parts of Iran, notably Fereidan near Isfahan, to which they were deported early in the seventeenth century by Shah 'Abbas I.

The Georgians refer to themselves as *Kartvel-ebi*, their homeland being called *Sa-kartvel-o*. Both these names are linked with that of a mythical demigod named Kartlos, 'ancestor' of the Georgian people; the principal province of central Georgia, in which Tbilisi (Tiflis) is situated, is called Kartli. As often occurs with ethnic terms, foreign nations have applied to the Georgians names which have no relation to their own collec' tive name of *Kartvel*. Thus, the Armenians and ancient Per' sians called the Georgians of the Eastern region *Virk* or *Wyrshn* respectively, the *vir* element giving rise to the name *Iveroi* or Iberians, used by the Greeks and Romans. Strabo and other Classical geographers, accustomed to thinking of the Iberians as denizens of Spain, were disconcerted to find other 'Iberians' living in the Caucasus, and invented theories that the country had once been settled by immigrants from Spanish Iberia. There are similarities between the Caucasian languages and Basque which might seem to give some support to this idea, though it cannot be seriously maintained in the light of modern scholarship. Very likely the root *vir* or *ber* has something to do with the ancient Caucasian tribes of the Sasperoi and Tibareni, prominent in the time of Herodotus. The Arabs and modern Persians call the Georgians 'Kurj' or 'Gurj'. From these forms the Western Europeans coined the name 'Georgians', which they went on to explain, quite incorrectly, as derived from that of St George, the country's patron and protector.

It is interesting that a similar confusion exists in the case of the neighbouring Albanians of the Caucasus, who formerly lived in the area now comprising Soviet Azerbaijan. These Caucasian Albanians have been extinct as a separate nation since the eleventh century AD. Their name is connected with the Armenian *Aghuan* or *Alvan*, and has absolutely nothing to do with the present'day Albanians of the Adriatic, next door to Yugoslavia. These modern Albanians emerge into history several centuries later than those of the Caucasus; they speak an Indo'European language, and in any case do not refer to themselves as Albanians at all, but 'Shqipetar'. Unless other' wise specified, all references in this volume to 'Iberians' and 'Albanians' refer to those who were indigenous inhabitants of the Caucasian isthmus, and not to those of the Mediterranean area.

From an anthropological viewpoint, the Georgians with the Svans and Mingrelo-Laz belong to the so-called 'Ponto-Zagros' group, occupying an intermediate position within the palaeo-Caucasian family of peoples. The contemporary Georgians are largely brachycephalic or hyperbrachycephalic, though according to Debets, the physical type has undergone considerable modification over the past two millennia. Most Georgians have fair, sallow or ruddy complexions and dark hair, though blondes also occur. Hazel-eyed for the most part, about thirty per cent have blue or grey eyes. In build, the Georgians are often above average height, well built, athletic and wiry. The people of the eastern provinces of Kartli and Kakheti tend to have prominent hooked noses and high, domed crania, whereas in Western Georgia, a straight, thin nose is more common, together with a physiognomy resembling the Mediterranean facial type of Southern Italy or Greece. Like the Armenians and also the Anatolian peasantry of today, the Georgians represent the result of several millennia of ethnic mingling. In the course of this process, the aboriginal, autochthonous substratum was overlaid by a number of successive waves of invading groups. In the case of the Armenians, whose language is classed as Indo-European, the Hurrian, Urartian physical type still shows through the Indo-Aryan overlay; in modern Turkey, a high-domed, hook-nosed physical type is still seen, having nothing in common with the slit-eyed Turkic nomadic peoples of the Altai, but considerable resemblance to figures depicted on ancient Hittite friezes. The greater remoteness of Georgia from the main paths of ancient invasion routes led to a greater demographic continuity, so that the Georgians of today may be taken as descended from autochthonous

denizens of the Caucasian isthmus and adjoining areas imme/
diately to the south/west, though with admixture of elements
from the Indo/European infiltration of the third millennium,
followed by the incursions of the Scythians and Cimmerians,
the settlements of the Milesian Greeks, and still later, the waves
of Arab, Mongol, Turkish and Persian conquerors. The cor/
porate life of the Georgian nation has its roots in the era of the
Hittites, Urartu and Assyria; unlike these vanished civiliza/
tions, that of Georgia has survived intact right up to the present
time.

The modern Georgian Soviet Socialist Republic covers an
area of 69,300 square kilometres; this includes the Abkhazian
Autonomous Republic with its capital of Sukhumi (the
ancient Dioscurias) on the Black Sea, the Ajar or Atchar
Autonomous Republic, with its capital Batumi, and the South
Ossetian Autonomous District centred on Tskhinvali, the one/
time Staliniri. The Ajars are simply Muslim Georgians, who
adopted Islam during several centuries of Ottoman rule; the
Abkhaz on the other hand are connected with the ancient
Heniochi, and belong to the North/Western or Adyghe/
Circassian group of Caucasian peoples, while the Ossetes are
descendants of the medieval Alans, an Indo/Iranian people
connected with the Sarmatians. Any historical study of the
Georgian people must also include within its purview a large
strip of the south/eastern shore of the Black Sea, known as
Lazistan, extending to Trebizond and further west, as well as
the upper Chorokhi valley as far as Bayburt and the areas around
the fortress towns of Kars and Ardahan and south/westwards
to Erzerum. Prior to the Seljuk invasions of the eleventh
century, this mountainous Pontic region, now within the
republic of Turkey, played a central role in the cultural,
linguistic and ethnic development of the Georgian nation.
At a still earlier epoch, the Meshech and Tubal of the Old
Testament, formidable tribes in central Anatolia, formed an

Fig. 1. Characteristic types of Georgian traditional houses: (1) Tower house of Svaneti mountaineers; (2) Eastern Georgian darbazi house; (3) Mingrelian circular thatched hut (patskha); (4) Western Georgian family home; (5) Tbilisi town house

important link between the Transcaucasian area and the ancient civilizations of Syria and Palestine.

Geographical and climatic conditions in Georgia are extremely varied. Of the territory of the modern Georgian Soviet Republic, some 54 per cent is mountainous, 33 per cent is occupied by hills and plateau land, only 13 per cent by plains and valleys. This diversity is reflected in the climate, which ranges from humid, subtropical conditions prevailing along the Black Sea littoral, through the drier, warm Mediterranean-type climate of inland Imereti and Kartli to the subalpine pastures and woods of the Caucasian uplands, themselves surmounted by the lofty, snow-capped peaks of Kazbek and Elbruz. A wide variety of fauna and flora is found in Georgia, a land which since the dawn of civilization has been found ideal for hunting, the raising of flocks and herds, wine growing, and many forms of agriculture. The country is rich in metals and minerals. Greek mythology, references in the Old Testament, and the massive testimony of archaeological research combine to show that Transcaucasia was one of the most ancient and renowned centres of mining and metallurgy. Minerals exploited in Georgia now include coal, manganese, oil, copper, iron, arsenic, wolfram, gold, marble, barite, lithographic stone, agate and mercury. Rivers, rich in fish, provide an abundant source of hydro-electric power, as well as the means of reclaiming and irrigating scarce arable land.

Fig. 1

Within a confined geographic area, the Georgians retain a number of well differentiated regional cultures and dialects. The Kartvelians—as the Georgians call themselves—early divided up along linguistic lines into three main groupings, the Iberians or Georgians proper, the Svans, and the Mingrelo-Laz. The Mingrelians and Laz became concentrated along the subtropical littoral of the Black Sea, the Svans formed independent tribal enclaves in the high Caucasus mountain valleys, while the dominant Ibero-Georgians occupied the modern provinces

Plate 1

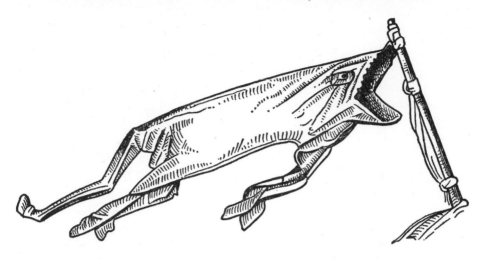

Fig. 2. Svanian 'lion' standard. Would become inflated during the cavalry onrush, to strike terror into the foe

of Kartli, Kakheti, Samtskhe, Imereti and certain adjoining
areas. Two thousand years ago, Strabo speaks of the Svans as
a powerful fighting nation capable of putting 200,000 warriors
in the field; nowadays, the entire body of Svanian speakers
numbers no more than 25,000. During the Arab domination
of Caucasia, many Georgian-speakers emigrated westward over
the Surami pass into ancient Colchis, driving a wedge across
the Rioni delta region to the Black Sea, and cutting off the
Mingrelians from physical contact with the cognate Laz population to the south.

Fig. 2

Georgian, Svanian and Mingrelo-Laz together constitute the
Ibero-Caucasian group within the Caucasian family of languages. Georgian is a highly flexible and complex tongue, of
great interest to philologists. The Caucasian languages are, of
course, entirely separate and distinct from the Indo-European,
Turkish and Semitic families, though in process of time many
words and constructions have been borrowed from these. It is
interesting, for instance, to find in Georgian the term *ghvino*
'wine', which some take to be an ancient borrowing from

23

Indo-European, while others regard it as evidence that Georgia was the primordial home of viticulture. Certain basic affinities can be traced between Old Georgian and Classical Armenian, which developed side by side, and share a common Anatolian, possibly Hurrian sub-stratum.

In view of widespread misconceptions, a word must be said about the term 'Caucasian' itself. Certain physical anthropologists who should know better, and also American immigration authorities who cannot be expected to do so, habitually use this word to denote virtually anyone who is not a Negro, a Jew, Indian, Chinese—in fact, as the virtual opposite of 'Coloured'. In short, a 'Caucasian' in this context comes to be the White Man *par excellence*, so that the term has taken on something of the meaning which in Hitler's time attached to 'Aryan'. This is utterly unscientific, and a complete misnomer. The Anglo-Saxons, Latins, Slavs and others to whom the term is so loosely applied have absolutely no historical or ethnic connexion with the Caucasian peoples proper, except for certain recent waves of immigration. For this reason, the term 'Caucasian' is used in this book solely to denote the ancient nations and tribes who have lived from time immemorial in the Caucasian isthmus and adjacent areas, the most important, apart from the Georgians themselves, being the Circassians, Kabardians and Abkhazians in the north-west, and the Checheno-Ingush, also the Avars, Lezghians and other peoples of Daghestan, in the north-east.

The position has also been complicated by the so-called 'Japhetic' theory associated with the name of Academician Nikolai Yakovlevich Marr (1864–1934). In his early days, Marr was a linguist and literary scholar of genius, who did an immense amount to make accessible the unknown treasures of ancient Georgian and Armenian civilization. Extending his researches further, into Asia Minor and the Mediterranean region, he had the idea of analyzing many obscure features of the prehistory of that area in terms of Caucasian languages and archaeology. He evolved the view, not unsound in itself, that many unexplained aspects of Mediterranean civilization repre׳ sented elements left over from a sub׳stratum more ancient than that of the Indo׳Europeans and the Semites—in short, from a 'third ethnic element', which he termed for convenience 'Japhetic', after Noah's third son Japhet, ancestor of Tubal and Meshech. After the Russian Revolution of 1917, Marr lost all moderation and evolved a highly fantastic system of his own, known as the 'New Teaching on Language'. All languages of the world were stated to be derived from four 'mystic' elements, *sal*, *ber*, *rosh* and *yon*, which Marr claimed to have had revealed to him in a dream. It is amazing that this phantasmagoria, masquerading as an offshoot of orthodox Marxism, should have won acceptance and been accepted as infallible in Russia for many years, until denounced by Stalin in 1950 and abandoned.

The phonemic system of Georgian comprises five cardinal vowels, but without any differentiation between short and long; there are twenty׳eight consonant phonemes. Old Georgian has two more consonants, and also diphthongs, which have since been reduced to single vowels. Georgian shares with North Caucasian languages some characteristic traits, notably the division of stops and affricates into three modes of articulation:

Fig. 3

(a) voiced: b, d, g, dz, j
(b) voiceless with aspiration: p', t', k', ts, ch
(c) voiceless, glottalised: p, t, k and q, ds, tch

Georgian has roughly the same parts of speech as most Indo׳ European languages, but possesses distinctive agglutinative and inflectional characteristics. The noun has seven cases: nomina׳ tive, vocative, genitive, dative׳accusative, ablative׳instrumental, adverbial, and ergative, this last being a special case form used for the agent in transitive verbs in the aorist tense and in certain other contexts. Instead of prepositions, Georgian employs post-positions. Often the fusion of the postposition with its noun gives the misleading appearance of secondary local cases, as where Old Georgian *mt'asa zeda* 'on the mountain' (literally: 'to mountain, on top') becomes Modern Georgian *mt'aze* 'mountain-on', and in many other such instances. The Old Georgian plural was formed by adding the suffix -*ni*, in oblique cases -*t'a*; Modern Georgian adds to the singular the plural suffix -*ebi*, plus the appropriate singular case endings where required. Georgian has no definite or indefinite article, nor any distinction of gender, even in the case of pronouns. Adjectives, which in Modern Georgian normally precede their noun, agree partially with the noun in case, but not in number; in Old Georgian, full agreement is the rule, and the adjective can follow the noun.

Most complicated of all is the Georgian verb, which is essentially multipersonal. Different rules govern the conjugation of transitive and intransitive, as well as the so-called 'middle' and 'indirect' verbs. According to the tense involved, the grammatical subject of a transitive verb may be in the nominative, the dative-accusative or the ergative case, while the object will be in the dative-accusative or the nominative. The Georgian verb is well adapted to distinguish between an action in progress, an action contemplated, an action completed once for all, and an action performed habitually. By use of appropriate vowel infixes, it can convey the idea of causation or compulsion, of an act performed to or for a third party, of an act performed for the benefit of the agent, and so on. Special prefixes are used to denote the spatial direction of an action or process, notably in the case of verbs of motion. Consonant prefixes and suffixes denote whether the agent is in the first, second or third person singular or plural; the direct object may also be specified in like manner. All this can prove rather baffling for the Anglo-Saxon student. Nor is a foreigner's difficulty dispelled by the Georgian

Ⴌ	ა	a	Ⴌ	ნ	n	Ⴕ	ყ	q
Ⴅ	ბ	b	Ⴆ	ჲ	y	Ⴣ	შ	š [sh]
Ⴐ	გ	g	Ⴍ	ო	o	Ⴠ	ჩ	č [ch]
Ⴃ	დ	d	Ⴎ	პ	p	Ⴚ	ც	c [ts]
Ⴄ	ე	e	Ⴕ	ჟ	ž [zh]	ქ	ძ	dz
Ⴇ	ვ	v	Ⴏ	რ	r	Ⴛ	ჳ	ç [ds]
Ⴆ	ზ	z	Ⴑ	ს	s	Ⴝ	ჭ	č [tch]
Ⴈ	ჱ	ey	Ⴒ	ტ	t	Ⴞ	ხ	ḫ [kh]
Ⴋ	თ	tᶜ	Ⴖ	უ	u	Ⴗ	ჴ	ḣ [kh]
Ⴉ	ი	i	Ⴣ	ჳ	w [vi]	Ⴘ	ჯ	j
Ⴊ	კ	k	Ⴔ	ფ	pᶜ	Ⴕ	ჳ	h
Ⴋ	ლ	l	Ⴕ	ქ	kᶜ	Ⴥ	ჵ	ho [oy]
Ⴌ	მ	m	Ⴍ	ღ	ġ [gh]			

Fig. 3. The Georgian alphabet showing: First column, the majuscule form of the ecclesiastical (khutsuri) script; second column, the mkhedruli *or modern alphabet; third column, the phonetic values*

language's exuberant clusters of consonants, as in *me vbrdsqinav* 'I shine', *khrdsna* 'to corrupt', or *pᶜrtskᶜvnis* 'he or she peels', which the native speaker takes in his stride. However, with its expressive sonority and rich vocabulary, the Georgian language in the mouth of a poet or orator can produce very splendid effects.

In their individual attitudes and social life, the Georgians have developed over the centuries certain quite distinctive traits, some of them shared with neighbouring peoples as part of a common Caucasian heritage of honour, hospitality and clan loyalty, others linked specifically with national temperament and the ancient traditions of the Georgian nation. Compared with their Russian and Muslim neighbours, the Georgians stand out by their proud, even flamboyant bearing, based on a conviction of the superiority of their own culture and achieve-ments. It has been said, in fact, that in Georgia every peasant is a prince, or behaves like one. They are strong in their personal and political opinions, excellent orators, passionate devotees of argument and intrigue. They excel as horsemen, marksmen and guerilla fighters, as herdsmen and growers and drinkers of wine. They are less adapted to life in a modern industrial community and do not always take kindly to factory or office work, or rou-tine occupations where personal initiative finds insufficient out-let. In contrast to Muslim traditions, the Georgians have always accorded a high place to women in their community life. This fact is symbolized by the special cults accorded to the Virgin Mary, to Saint Nino, the Apostle of Georgia, and to Queen Tamar, symbol of Georgia's Golden Age. Though subjected to chaperonage and other restraints, Georgian women have never been accustomed to wearing veils in public or to being excluded from the general run of social and public life. Quick to resent insult and respond to courtesy, Georgians take pride in dispensing hospitality on a scale often in excess of what they can properly afford. A people who have produced great poets, dancers and musicians, they relish the good things of life and human fellowship. Easy-going, even epicurean in their approach to life, Georgians are gifted with lively intelligence and a ready sense of humour. Like the Armenians, they have consistently produced a large intelligentsia, with a high quota of professors, doctors, teachers, civil servants, army officers and professional men generally; in commercial acumen, however, they lag behind, sometimes failing to draw the full benefit from their own country's rich natural resources. 'Relaxed, fierce and full of joy', as one Western traveller has termed them, the Georgians are stimulating company, though they can some-times baffle those who attempt unbidden to penetrate the inner world of their individual and close-knit national society.

.   .   .

Until quite recently, virtually nothing was known of the existence of human life in Georgia prior to the Bronze Age. Distinguished early scholars like Jacques de Morgan could doubt whether any Palaeolithic or Neolithic cultures existed there at all. Archaeological discoveries during the last half century have radically altered our concept of Georgia's prehistory. In particular, it is no longer possible to conceive, as some earlier scholars tended to do, of a 'proto-Georgian' civilization created entire outside the historical boundaries of Georgia and then imported in the course of some *Völkerwanderung* or mass migration of peoples into a land virtually vacant and uninhabited. Today, archaeological evidence points rather to Georgia being among those lands which witnessed the birth of human life on our planet. The habitation and evolution of mankind and man's productive techniques and social organization continued within the territory of Georgia throughout the major epochs of prehistory and recorded time. Whatever role extraneous influences, races and cultures—and there were many—played in forming the Georgian nation and its ancient civilization, these elements must themselves have been superimposed upon ancient, autochthonous populations and cultural patterns existing in the Caucasus since the dawn of human life itself.

In this connexion, it is perhaps relevant to note that the Garesja desert region, east of Tbilisi, is the site of the discovery of remains of a distinctive variety of anthropoid ape, the so-called Udabnopithecus (from Georgian *udabno*, 'a wilderness'). This creature occupied an intermediary position between the chimpanzee and the gorilla. The discovery was made in 1939 by Soviet geologists N. O. Burchak-Abramovich and E. G. Gabashvili. The remains are extremely fragmentary—two teeth, one being a molar—but they represent the only ancient anthropoid ape remains found on the territory of the U.S.S.R. Some Soviet scholars regard this discovery as evidence that Transcaucasia was among the regions of the world where the transition from ape to *homo sapiens* took place at the close of the Tertiary and the beginning of the Pleistocene epoch.

However this may be, the presence of Stone Age man in Georgia from Lower Palaeolithic times onwards is attested by scores of important finds, centred for the most part on the Rioni (Phasis) valley and the seaboard of Abkhazia. Since 1914, when R. Schmidt and L. Kozlovsky carried out the first systematic investigation of Stone Age settlements in Georgia and discovered flint artifacts of the Aurignacian culture in Sakazhia cave near Motsameti on the left bank of the River Dsqaldsitela, Russian and Georgian archaeologists have explored a large number of open and cave Palaeolithic sites, extending our chronological horizon steadily farther back and providing new and significant material for the study of early phases of human life on our planet. In 1958 an expedition of the Georgian Academy of Sciences headed by Nino Berdzenishvili located implements of the Abbevillian (Chellean) culture at a site in Abkhazia, close to the north-eastern shores of the Black Sea. This discovery provides a link with the Satani-dar (Satan's Hill) finds of obsidian implements made in 1946–48 by Sardaryan and Panichkina in the vicinity of Mount Bogatlu in Armenia, and usually regarded as the most ancient of all archaeological remains discovered in the Soviet Union.

The Acheulian culture is particularly well represented in Georgia and adjoining regions. In 1934–36, an expedition led by Sergei Zamyatnin (1899–1958) discovered an important group of some ten sites of this epoch along the Abkhazian coast of the Black Sea. These sites are mainly between Gagra and the mouth of the River Inguri. When the people of the Acheulian culture settled here, the level of the Black Sea was nearly 200 feet higher than today. For this reason, some of the most significant finds, such as those made at Yashtkhva, 3 kilometres north of Sukhumi, have been made on seaboard terraces between 200 and 300 feet above the present sea-level. Subsequently, Acheulian settlements have also been located at Lashe-Balta in Southern Ossetia, an inland region immediately to the south of the main Caucasian chain.

Our knowledge of early human life in Georgia broadens considerably when we reach the Mousterian—a term used by Soviet archaeologists to include all epochs and cultures dated from between about 100,000 and 40,000 BC, which Western scholars usually prefer to group more loosely under the name of 'Middle Palaeolithic'. Kerd'l lists twenty-five Mousterian sites on or near the Black Sea coast of Abkhazia and Mingrelia (the ancient Colchis), as well as five in the Rioni valley and twenty in the vicinity of the River Kura (Mtkvari) and its tributaries. Of particular interest are the four palaeolithic cave settlements discovered by V. P. Lyubin at Kudaro, high in the mountains of South Ossetia. In Kudaro I, Mousterian culture layers cover remains of prior Acheulian habitation, evidently of long duration. Bones of a wide variety of fauna recovered at Kudaro include those of the huge and formidable cave bear, comprising as much as three-quarters of the total, also stag, roe-buck, bison, wild sheep, wild goat, red wolf, wolf, fox, wolverine, panther, boar, marten, field mouse, bat, and the occasional macaco. The Mousterian layers contained remains of rhinoceros, chamois, marmot, badger, mole, otter, hamster, hare and weasel. Finds of artifacts recently made in the vicinity of Samshvilde have established further that Mousterian camping sites existed in Lower Kartli, along the basin of the River Khrami, a tributary of the Mtkvari.

No less important in the prehistory of Georgia is the Upper Palaeolithic period, extending approximately from 40,000 to 12,000 BC. This coincided with the late glacial epoch, when climatic severity reached its peak and tundra and cold steppe conditions invaded vast expanses of the world. Transition to the Upper Palaeolithic stage was marked by important changes in the life of primitive people. New techniques, new forms of domestic economy made their appearance, and changes took place in social organization and also in the physical features of man himself. The human types that emerged no longer had semi-simian features; they walked erect and had the hands of modern human beings. The working of flint was considerably improved. In the Mousterian period, cores were disc-shaped, while the flakes struck from them were triangular; now, disc-shaped cores were replaced by prismatic cores with regular faces, enabling longer, thinner, knife-shaped flakes to be struck from them. Bones, antlers and mammoth tusks supplemented flint and obsidian as material for tools and weapons. The bow and arrow was invented. Shapes of certain stone and bone objects show that they were originally fitted with wooden handles. Though hunting and the gathering of fruits and berries remained the chief form of Upper Palaeolithic man's economic activity and means of subsistence, improved techniques and a higher level of productivity gradually enabled him to pass to a more settled and sophisticated way of life. Permanent dwellings were built or hollowed out, religious beliefs arose, and cave-painting and sculpture reached a new pitch of refinement. Where caves were lacking, artificial protection against the cold was provided by tents made of skins, and even by substantial 'houses', dug in the soft loess soil and roofed by hides and turfs. Palaeolithic houses of this kind were common in Russia (Push-kari, Gagarino, Kostyenki) and Siberia (Buret, Mal'ta), where natural shelters were scarcer than in the Caucasus mountains; now traces of such habitations are also coming to light in Georgia.

Among the first Upper Palaeolithic remains to be found in Georgia are those described in 1916 by S. Krukovsky, from the cave of Gvarjilasklde near Rgani village in the Chiatura district of Imereti. These materials are assigned to the upper layer of the Magdalenian culture. Subsequently, outstanding work on the Upper Palaeolithic in Georgia was done by Giorgi

Nioradze (1886–1951), author of a fine monograph on the Aurignacian cave-camp of Devis-Khvreli, 4 kilometres from Kharagouli in the Shorapani district, also in Imereti (Western Georgia). Besides animal bones, a human jaw bone and many flint implements were found in Devis-Khvreli, enabling Nioradze to make an impressive reconstruction of the entire way of life of Upper Palaeolithic man in Georgia. In 1936, Nioradze renewed the investigations at Sakazhia cave near Motsameti (not far from Kutaisi, capital of Imereti) begun by Schmidt and Kozlovsky in 1914, and came up with fresh discoveries, including bones of the cave bear and cave lion, elk and bison, fragments of human skulls, and abundant remains of mineral paints.

Palaeolithic cave drawings are of course extremely rare in the U.S.S.R., and not to be compared with those of France and Spain. A certain interest attaches to those discovered in the Mghvimevi caves near Chiatura, comprising symbols of a geometric, linear character. It is also worth noting that finds unearthed in 1951–53 at Sagvarjile near Dzevri in the Terzhola district by N. Z. Kiladze and other scientists from Tbilisi include primitive carved bone implements, such as an awl depicting a fish with a herring-bone ornament on its tail, also pendants, a bone pin, and a necklace of perforated sea-shells.

Regarding the social organization of primitive man in Georgia and elsewhere, Soviet scholars led by M. O. Kosven believe that the Upper Palaeolithic witnessed the formation of the institution of 'Matriarchate', or the matriarchal clan system, which also continued throughout the Mesolithic and Neolithic periods. The succeeding Eneolithic or Chalcolithic epoch, according to this theory, was marked by transition to the dominance of the male elder or clan leader, that is, the patriarchal system. This whole question remains highly speculative.

The onset of a new epoch, the Neolithic or New Stone Age, took place in the post-glacial period, when weather grew warmer and conditions generally more temperate. During the transitional Mesolithic period, reckoned to extend from approximately 12,000 to 5000 BC, men emerged from their dank cave-dwellings or cosy dug-outs, as the case might be, and exchanged the troglodytic way of life for a more mobile outdoor existence, though cave sites and artificial dwellings were retained in use for the winter or as refuges in time of trouble. Because of his semi-nomadic way of life, physical traces of Mesolithic man tend to be dispersed and lost, though there are some interesting examples in Georgia, such as the lower layer at the Odishi camping site, near Zugdidi in Mingrelia, explored by A. N. Kalandadze in 1936–37. The Odishi Mesolithic finds include a number of microliths, of a type comparable to that characteristic of Iran and Iraq.

The fifth and fourth millennia BC witnessed the emergence in Georgia and adjoining regions of a Neolithic culture, having numerous points of resemblance with the Neolithic of the Mediterranean area, Asia Minor and the Crimea. Characteristic implements include chipped and polished stone axes with a slightly curved handle, and smoothly finished implements in the form of gouges and chisels. Besides the Odishi site already mentioned, Neolithic settlements are located on the Black Sea coast, at Tetramidsa near Kutaisi, and also in Eastern Georgia. The Neolithic inhabitants of Georgia were hunters, fishermen and food gatherers; they were also grain farmers, as attested by finds of stone hand-mills, flint flakes with little teeth that served as blades for wooden sickles, also stone hoes and mattocks. In Colchis, agriculture reached an advanced stage, millet, wheat and barley being among cereal crops grown. Stores of chestnuts, acorns and hazel nuts and accumulations of grape pips have been found in settlements at Reka and Anaklia. From discoveries at Kistrika near Gudauti in Abkhazia, we know that the womenfolk were by now spinning and knitting rudimentary garments. Primitive pottery also makes its appearance. From

Odishi, Kalandadze recovered remains of Neolithic handmade ceramic ware, with ornamental motifs in the form of broken or wavy, occasionally also zigzag lines. Weak in technique and crude in design, this early Transcaucasian pottery evidently represents an offshoot of the superior Neolithic ceramic culture of Anatolia, which was already flourishing around 6000 BC. Animal husbandry also was an important branch of Neolithic life in Georgia, as attested by finds of bones of oxen, cows, sheep, goats and tame dogs, showing that several kinds of animals were already widely domesticated here as in other regions of Caucasia.

CHAPTER II

Copper and Bronze

A MAJOR BREAK-THROUGH in the study of Georgian and Transcaucasian prehistory has occurred during the last few decades, with the discovery of widespread remains of what is variously called the 'Encolithic culture of Transcaucasia' (Munchaev, Piotrovsky), the 'Chalcolithic and early Bronze Age culture of Eastern Anatolia' (Burney), the 'Transcaucasian Copper Age Culture' (Gimbutas) or the 'Kuro-Araxes culture' (Kushnareva, Chubinishvili and others). In Chalcolithic cultures such as this, the cold-forging of copper proceeded side by side with the making of axes and other implements by means of stone moulds; but in view of the malleability of copper, flint was still retained in use for many purposes. To this day, primordial memories of the Caucasian Copper Age live on in oral legend and folklore, as in the Abkhazian tradition whereby there lived in the Caucasus in remote antiquity the first smith of all, who used his fist for a hammer, his knee for an anvil, and fashioned all manner of objects by hand from unalloyed copper.

The bulk of our material on the Transcaucasian Chalcolithic or Copper Age culture comes from tell and hilltop settlements in Armenia (for instance, Shengavit, near Erevan), from present-day Soviet Azerbaijan, from Georgia (Trialeti, Tbilisi area, Gori, Samtskhe province, also Samtredia and other parts of Imereti), and even from mountainous Daghestan (Kayakent). During the first quarter of the third millennium BC, when the Caucasus emerged from isolation to become an integral part of the larger Near Eastern world, not only the manufacture of metals but the entire level of material culture in Transcaucasia underwent great improvement. This was due to development of large-scale commercial contacts and exchange of technological processes between the Caucasian tribes and the great civilizations of the ancient Near East.

This Kuro-Araxes, Chalcolithic or Copper Age culture can be dated with some precision by means of Carbon-14 analysis of selected samples from the Nakhchevan Kül-Tepe, where the Chalcolithic stratum at a depth of 8·5 metres gave a result of 4880±90, while a comparable sample from Kvatskhelebi near Urbnisi in Kartli gave the result 4760±90. Tariel Chubinish-vili dates the important Chalcolithic settlement of Amiranis-gora near Akhaltsikhe in south-western Georgia to the period 3000 to 2700 BC.

The villages of this period were made up of rectangular, round or oval houses, with mud brick walls. Stone, wood and reeds were also used as building materials. More recently, elon-gated buildings with rounded corners have been discovered at Chalcolithic sites in Inner Kartli. They might be regarded as a combination of round and square plans, not unlike Thessalian oval houses. Economic life was based on farming and stock raising, with emphasis on the rearing of cattle, sheep, goats, dogs and horses. Clay figurines of oxen, rams, barking dogs and horses appear in abundance, pointing to the prevalence of various forms of animal worship, accompanied by sacrifices and other ritual observances. Cattle raising developed rapidly, and the stock farming of the period is documented by quanti-ties of domestic animal bones. Agriculture centred on grain and orchard crops and mixed plantings; harvesting and flour-making implements are found in large numbers. Some toy models of oxen have small hollows in the fore part of the trunk, showing that they were designed to be attached to model carts, the clay wheels of which, with projecting hubs, have in fact been preserved. There were also the usual conventional female figurines. Other interesting finds include archaic shaft-hole 'battle-axes', tube-socketed copper axeheads, and pear-shaped sceptre-heads of polished stone. Fragments of a milk-churn found at Dablagomi show that milk and dairy products formed part of the diet of Eneolithic man in Georgia. Fishing was carried on systematically in rivers, lakes and in the Black Sea with the aid of well-made nets, kept in place with stone weights.

A major, indeed quite sensational feature of the Transcaucasian Kuro-Araxes culture of the third millennium BC is its distinctive hand-made pottery, painted black or red and burnished to a high metallic gloss. The vessels are commonly decorated with grooved, geometric ornament and are sometimes of eccentric shape, cups for instance being found with bases so small and tapering that it is hard to make them stand upright. Research by Soviet and Western archaeologists shows conclusively that this Kuro-Araxes ware is virtually identical with that found in Syria and Palestine and called 'Khirbet Kerak', after the village of that name, the ancient Beth-Yerah, situated at the south-west corner of the Sea of Galilee, where this pottery was first located. In Albright's view (*Archaeology of Palestine*, p. 76), this is some of the most beautiful pottery ever made in Palestine, where it was in use from about 2600 to 2400 BC, driving out of fashion the regular, wheel-made pottery already long typical of those parts. A few sherds from Jericho identified by G. M. FitzGerald, and others from Lachish (Tell el-Duweir), show that the Khirbet Kerak ware spread down into southern Palestine before finally petering out. Several authorities, including Kathleen Kenyon and Ruth Amiran, conclude that the Khirbet Kerak ware was brought to Syria and Palestine by some invading group from eastern Anatolia or beyond—'barbarous tribes', as V. Gordon Childe (*New Light on the Most Ancient East*, p. 219) surmises, 'coming perhaps from Georgia'. It was not carried there by the current of normal trade relations; in Syria, its appearance is accompanied by disturbances suggesting actual invading groups. The invaders chose to ignore the well-established potteries of Syria, where the technique of the potter's wheel was so well known, and went on for generations fashioning by hand their exotic vessels in an alien style, until they were finally absorbed or driven out. Who were these intrusive Khirbet Kerak potters? They may have been an early wave of Hurrians, a people later so important in the history of Syria and northern Mesopotamia; there is every likelihood that they were ethnically connected with the ancestors of the Georgians and related tribal group-ings. At all events, it is significant that Georgia and Armenia, central and eastern Anatolia, even Daghestan and Checheno-Ingushetia to the north of the main Caucasian range, are all characterized by finds of pottery closely similar to Khirbet Kerak-type ware—a fact which testifies to a phase of intense cultural and ethnic interpenetration during the middle of the third millennium BC of peoples dwelling on the fringes of the Mediterranean Sea right up to the Black Sea and the Caucasus mountains, a process in which the forerunners of the Georgian nation were intimately involved.

Recent pioneer work by Georgian archaeologists on several new sites sheds still further light on the Caucasian Chalco-lithic and Copper Age and the transition to Early Bronze. Besides Tariel Chubinishvili's monograph on Amiranis-gora in Meskheti (south-western Georgia), we have Otar Japaridze's fundamental study on the history of the Georgian tribes and their ancestors in the Chalcolithic and Early Bronze eras (1961; with English summary); this contains among other valuable material a synchronic chart of various kinds of Georgian pot-tery and the types of copper and primitive bronze weapons and implements associated with them thoughout the third millen-nium BC. Japaridze has studied in detail the Chalcolithic of Georgia's heartland, Inner Kartli, with special reference to the village of Kulbakebi near Tskhinvali (Staliniri) in South Ossetia. The Chalcolithic stratum at Kulbakebi was under a layer of stone, after the removal of which Chalcolithic ware was unearthed over the entire area. A round hearth was uncovered close to the centre; several flint sickle-blades were found, as well as a knife, some arrowheads and a celt. Kulbakebi pottery is noteworthy for elegance of form, good modelling and firing; it consists mostly of red polished ware. Two unusual three-handled vessels from Kulbakebi, together with another one from Ozni, are illustrated by Japaridze, who draws attention to a characteristic form of decoration on Georgian Chalco-lithic pottery, namely a pattern of spirals in relief. A widespread variant of this motif is a linked pair of spirals, something like a pair of spectacles.

Burials of various dates were unearthed at Kulbakebi. Par-ticular interest attaches to a metal axehead found by Lyubin, which resembles in shape a stone axe found at another Geor-gian site, Khizaant-gora, and an axe of gypsum cast in a mould which was discovered at Shengavit in Armenia. Axes with blades bending downwards to the shaft-hole were common in Georgia in the later Chalcolithic period. They resemble very archaic Mesopotamian axes known to us from clay models; as in Mesopotamia, axes of this type were soon superseded by the tube-socketed kind and disappeared from use. Towards the end of the Chalcolithic, metal was not only being cold-forged, but casting was by degrees coming into use, as shown by moulds from Shengavit, Kvatskhelebi and Kül-Tepe. By the close of the Georgian Chalcolithic, between 2400 and 2200 BC, all kinds of implements, including scythes and axeheads, spears and other weapons, are already being made of metal, specifically, copper containing an admixture of arsenic, the superior qualities of arsenical copper being already known to Georgian metal-workers.

The technical aspects of early metallurgy in Georgia are ably expounded in two other monographs published in Tbilisi, complete with English summaries, namely a book by Ts. N. Abesadze and others (1958), and another by Tavadze and Saqvarelidze (1959). Taken in conjunction with such works

Plate 6

as Forbes' *Metallurgy in Antiquity* (new edition, 1964), these excellent books, based on research carried out in the laboratory of the Georgian State Museum, enable us to build up a coherent picture of metal-working techniques in Georgia from the Chalcolithic era onwards. The Georgian scientists describe how, in the age when native copper was first employed, the primitive master came to know the properties of metal: its plasticity, malleability, its metallic ring, its characteristic glitter and smell, and other properties which distinguished it from stone. Subsequently he learnt to distinguish various metals and minerals from one another by their colouring; for instance, he distinguished copper from gold and silver. As the craftsman mastered the cold smithing of metals, he could use as prototypes in giving shape to his products various objects of stone, wood or bone already in use and familiar to him. Georgian native copper normally contains slightly over 1 per cent of arsenic. The transition between the Copper and the Early Bronze Age occurred when the master craftsman, having become familiar with the properties of metal, both hot and molten, and with the process of direct reduction of metal from complex, easily reducible ores, unintentionally obtained oligarsenide of copper, *i.e.*, low-grade arsenide bronze. Noticing that molten metal when cooling takes the shape of the vessel in which it is contained, the metal-worker would begin to fashion crude stone or clay moulds, and later, more perfect ones of wax. The making of wire also originated at this period. At first, all-round forging was employed; later on, wire is drawn. In this latter process, a drilled hard stone was used, jasper for preference.

Throughout the Early Bronze Age, the arsenic content of the copper/bronze alloy gradually increased, reaching about 6 per cent, thus proving that by now an arsenide of metal was being artificially introduced into the charge. By the Middle Bronze Age, many branches of advanced metal processing had been perfected in Georgia: casting, forging, chasing, cutting, stamping, grinding and polishing, also jewellery inlaying. Antimony bronze was commonly employed in the Middle Bronze Age throughout Georgia; in the Trialeti area, tin bronze is a special feature, tin deposits being found locally in a number of places. In Abkhazian dolmen finds, the antimony content reaches 12 per cent. During the Middle Bronze Age, both tin and antimony were used in the heartland of Inner Kartli to make bronze. Abesadze (1958; p. 108) makes a number of interesting deductions on the effects of the introduction of tin bronze into Georgian metallurgical processes. She writes:

It is characteristic that when tin came to be used, the content of arsenic in objects drops sharply, but still arsenic is always present. This leads us to suppose that arsenical copper ore was still the raw material employed, but the metallurgists tried to eliminate the arsenic. It is, of course, hard to say at present how this was achieved. We are of the opinion that before tin came to be used, oxidized copper ore was smelted in open furnaces with access of air. The greater part of the arsenic and antimony passed from the ore into the metal, a minor part went into the slag. The smelted metal containing arsenic, as compared to pure copper, was harder and easier to cast.

The further development of metallurgy brought mankind to the employment of tin. Simultaneously, sulphide ores came to be used along with oxidized ores. It may be surmised that smelting was effected in special vessels; a crucible of clay might have been employed and, with a view to raising the temperature and accelerating the process of smelting, it might have been covered with a lid. This may have been the transition from open smelting to closed smelting without access of air. Closed smelting caused a number of chemical reactions: under the influence of high temperatures, arsenic and antimony entered into compounds with sulphur; sulphides were formed which escaped as smoke. This process caused the elimination of large amounts of arsenic and antimony. Insignificant amounts of these elements remained in the metal, which fact has many times been shown by analyses.

The Georgian scientists support their general deductions by analytical tables of the chemical composition of metal objects found in Transcaucasia, right up to the Late Bronze Age, as well as providing diagrams, formulae and other data of a technical nature. Their work thus affords a valuable adjunct to comparative study of early technology in the Near East and the ancient world generally.

The unity of the Chalcolithic and Early Bronze Age culture of eastern Anatolia and Transcaucasia breaks up towards the close of the third millennium, evidently under the impact of IndoEuropean invasion from the north Caucasian steppelands. These IndoEuropeans (assuming that they were such) were bearers of what Marija Gimbutas (*American Anthropologist*, 1963, p. 821) terms the Eurasian *kurgan* ('barrow') culture, represented by the Nalchik cemetery on the upper Terek. The Maikop period of this IndoEuropean *kurgan* culture, extending from about 2300 to 2100 BC, is famous for its royal graves at Maikop and Tsarskaya in the Kuban basin, with their mausoleums built of timber or of stone slabs, and furnished with a fantastic quantity of gold, silver and copper objects, pottery and stone vases, gold figurines of bulls and lions, gold beads and rings, also copper axes, daggers and spearheads, all showing close affinities with northern Iran and the royal tombs in central Anatolia. From this we must conclude that even prior to the efflorescence of this Maikop culture, *kurgan* groups had already crossed over the Caucasus mountains and penetrated the cultural milieux of Transcaucasia and Anatolia; this enabled them to adapt themselves to the standards of a higher civilization, which they then imparted to their own homelands in northern Caucasia. Indeed, similarities between the Maikop burials and those at Alaca Hüyük and Horoztepe have led more than one good authority, including Marija Gimbutas, to ascribe the Maikop culture to predecessors of the historically known Hittites, and to conclude that these proto-Hittites appeared in Anatolia via Georgia and Transcaucasia around 2000 BC. Other scholars, it must be said, continue to assert that the Hittites entered Anatolia from the West, and have nothing to do with other Indo-European influxes from northern Caucasia and the Eurasian steppes.

The arrival of the Indo-Europeans on the scene had far-reaching effects on the Early Bronze Age culture of Georgia and adjoining regions. It contributed notably to the formation of the magnificent local civilization centred on Trialeti, a district south-west of Tbilisi, watered by the River Khrami. The Trialeti Bronze Age culture developed out of the fusion of several different elements, some indigenous, some brought in from the steppes north of the Caucasian range, others deriving from the Araxes valley and ultimately from north-western Iran. This unique Trialeti culture is now well known through the excavations of M. M. Ivashchenko (1891–1946) and B. A. Kuftin (1892–1953), who uncovered more than forty huge burial mounds, the oldest of which—Barrow VIII—is dated approximately 2100 BC, while others continue in chronological sequence up to about the fifteenth century BC. These are the graves of chiefs and princes of rich pastoral tribes. Their cremated remains, sometimes reposing on or near a wooden oxen-drawn four-wheeled cart, would be deposited in great burial pits, up to twenty-five feet deep, accompanied by remains of cattle and sheep, beautiful painted pottery, and ornaments and vessels of gold and silver.

Plates 7, 9–11, 14

Each of these remarkable barrow tombs shelters one body only. The extreme rarity—in most of the *kurgans*, the complete

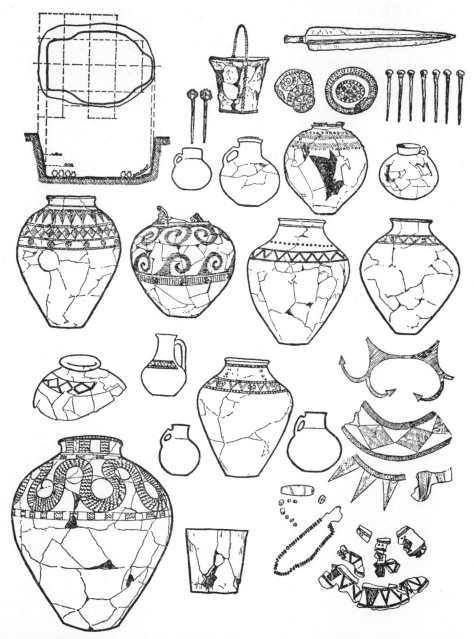

Fig. 4. Complete inventory of Kurgan XVII, Trialeti, c. 1500 BC. After Kuftin

Fig. 5. Bronze belt showing hunting scene. From Trialeti, c. 1500 BC. Length about 90 cm. State Museum of Georgia, Tbilisi

absence—of weapons shows that these are tombs of chiefs of a peaceable population. It was a people devoted to agriculture and the rearing of cattle, sheep, goats and pigs, whose bones are found among the offerings. In addition, it hunted the wild-goat, the ibex, the chamois, the roe-deer, the fallow-deer and the wild boar, whose shapes adorn some of the funerary vessels. Among the many animals sacrificed to the dead, the horse does not appear. As horses were used in the Caucasus at the time of the Trialeti *kurgans*, one must suppose, as C. F. A. Schaeffer (1944) points out, that there were religious or economic or sentimental taboos, forbidding its sacrifice at funerals. Schaeffer further draws a parallel with tombs of warriors of the La Tène period in France and southern Germany, where chariots were buried complete with harness, but horses themselves were sacrificed extremely seldom.

Fig. 4

The inventory of the Trialeti burials is varied and rich. There is a much damaged silver bucket, decorated with gold, entirely covered with embossed ornamentation figuring a Plate 11 variety of wild animals in a stylized forest; a silver goblet adorned with a religious scene and several goblets or cups of Plate 9 gold, one adorned with filigree spirals and granulation and studded with turquoises and carnelians set *en cabochon*. An

46

astonishing *situla* of beaten bronze, set on a hollow pedestal, from *Kurgan* XV, vividly recalls Early Iron Age bronze caul-drons from Italy. A bronze socketed spearhead, with a silver ferrule, also from *Kurgan* XV, resembles a similar example from Ras Shamra, dating from between 1550 and 1400 BC, and others from an intact grave at Kephalari near Mycenae of approximately the same date. From these Trialeti grave goods, it can be clearly seen that Georgian artisans of the Middle Bronze Age used all kinds of complex equipment and tools—a

Figs. 5, 6

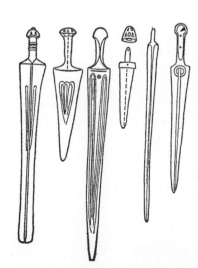

Fig. 6. Characteristic types of Trans-caucasian Bronze Age swords and daggers. After Iessen

Fig. 7. Painted vase from Trialeti. c. 1500 BC. Height 68 cm. State Museum of Georgia, Tbilisi

prototype of the turning lathe, the smelting furnace, the forge, the anvil, and a variety of cutters, dividers and casting appliances.

Fig. 7
Plate 14

Trialeti pottery with geometrical decoration of a very refined pattern is found in these burials along with vessels in grey or blackish burnished paste. Some of the painted vases have a shiny, whitish glaze, and are covered with a design in rich dark brown glossy paint. Frequent use of the spiral motif, alone or conjoined, already known from the Georgian Chalcolithic, also recalls the fondness for this pattern in the Mycenaean age. Another group of vessels is painted red all over, this being the ground for a black pattern of triangular shapes, arranged like petals round the neck and shoulders of the vases.

It must again be stressed that no extraneous forces could have brought about this remarkable upsurge in Georgia during the second millennium BC, had it not been for remarkable developments in local mining and metallurgy, which have their roots in the Transcaucasian Chalcolithic era. Not for nothing is Tubal-cain ('Tubal the smith'), son of Lamech and 'forger of all instruments of bronze and iron' (*Genesis* iv. 22), often

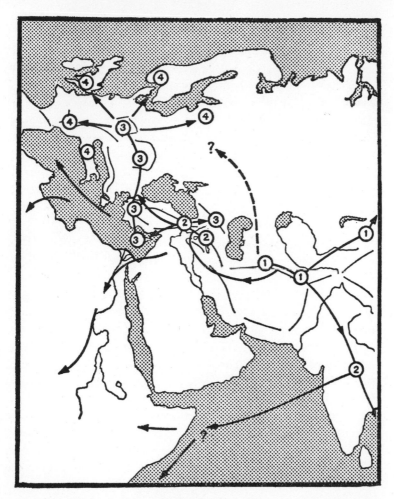

Fig. 8. The diffusion of early metallurgy. After Forbes. The numerals are an indication of the chronological sequence

associated with the legendary ancestors of the Georgian and Caucasian peoples. Henri Frankfort and V. Gordon Childe, after careful examination of evidence from the Aegean, from Anatolia and from northern Persia, have lent their support to the concept of an ancient cradle of metallurgy in Transcaucasia,

Fig. 8

while R. J. Forbes, in his sketch map of the diffusion of early metallurgical techniques, allots a central place to Georgia and Armenia. W. F. Albright once drew suggestive parallels between the Tubal-cain of Genesis, the Chalybes of the Moschian mountains, and the Babylonian god Ninurta, whose name could be interpreted alternatively as 'Lord of Armenia (Urartu)' or 'Lord of Iron'. Certainly Caucasia possessed not only copper ore in abundance, but also the necessary alloys, including antimony and tin, the latter occurring in Ratcha, South Ossetia, also near Shorapani, Gori, Borjomi and Ganja (Kirovabad).

Besides the fine Bronze Age culture of Trialeti, which is also connected with the Armenian *kurgan* civilization represented by sites such as Kirovakan, there existed also a distinctive Middle Bronze culture in western Georgia (Imereti), where investigations were begun by E. S. Taqaishvili in 1910. An interesting site here is that of Tsartsis-gora in the Sachkhere district, where clan cemeteries have preserved traces of a local civilization going back to late Chalcolithic times (2400–2200 BC), and continuing to flourish through the Middle Bronze Age. Gold ornaments from Sachkhere parallel objects from Troy II, while there are bronze axes with bent blades having clear Anatolian

Plate 6

affinities, as well as others of the tube-socketed type. Among metal ornaments from the Sachkhere mounds are large pins of two kinds: toggle-pins and racquet-pins. Later burials contain pins of another type, with the head shaped like ram's horns. Such pins have a wide distribution, from Troy to North Caucasia. Pottery from Sachkhere is mostly black with a pink slip. The wealth of this area of western Georgia was firmly based on several important local mining and metallurgical centres, such as that near the village of Gebi, on the upper reaches of the Rioni river, where Bronze Age antimony galleries and ore-smelting furnaces have been discovered, with numerous metal artifacts forged or cast from antimony bronze.

Fig. 9. Bronze Age dolmen tomb, from the Black Sea coastal region. After Tallgren

Further westwards, a highly interesting but as yet little known Bronze Age culture came into being towards the end of the third millennium BC along the Black Sea coast of Abkhazia, a region noted, we have seen, for the richness of its palaeolithic remains. This civilization, which extended through north-western Caucasia far towards the Crimea, is characterized by a large number of 'dolmen' burial structures, of which at least 1500 have so far been investigated. The best known complex of dolmens is at Esheri, between Sukhumi and Gudauti; though many of the dolmen graves were looted in antiquity, several still contained groups of skeletons together with burial objects in bronze. These Abkhazian dolmens are usually formed from five enormous blocks of stone, measuring up to 8 feet high by 12 feet long. The front block has an oval aperture, usually about 18 inches in diameter, serving the dual purpose of admitting fresh corpses and, presumably, of permitting the souls of the deceased to depart into the world to come. These apertures are commonly sealed up by a stone bung weighing 50 lb or more.

Fig. 9

Georgia, like Armenia, is generally rich in ancient megalithic structures. Besides dolmens, we find many great upright monoliths and also so-called cyclopean walls, made of huge, roughly-coursed blocks of stone without mortar. These structures preceded the building of regular townships, and were highly necessary to provide tribes and their livestock with protection during the clashes and migrations of peoples which were frequent in Transcaucasia during the Bronze Age. For this purpose, extensive ramparts of megaliths were built, usually spread over the slopes or summits of hills, sometimes as a group of linked compounds or enclosures, *e.g.* at Gokhnari, Avranlo and Santa, elsewhere constructed in the form of labyrinths, as at Lodovani. These fortified sites, laid out usually in the form of quadrangles, with cylindrical watch towers, enabled the people and their livestock to find refuge in times of trouble. In addition, the border region between Georgia and Armenia is rich in single free-standing vertical megaliths or *menhirs*, often carved with representations of animal or bird totems. Many of these probably belong to a period later than the Middle Bronze Age, and should be assigned to the first millennium BC, especially the conspicuous megaliths carved with the emblem of a fish or sea dragon—the so-called *vishaps*—often found on hillsides on the Armenian and Georgian borderlands. These *vishaps* were evidently associated in some way with ancient Urartian irrigation systems; they are found on high hills from which canals flowed down into the valleys, notably in the Trialeti and Ararat regions, both of which were densely populated from the Bronze Age onwards.

The Middle Bronze Age in Transcaucasia, which covers a substantial part of the second millennium BC, coincided with the rise of a new power in Anatolia, the Hittite empire. The Hittites kept detailed state records in their own highly developed form of cuneiform writing, and it might be hoped that the extensive archives of their kings would cast some light on events in the as yet pre-literate Transcaucasian area. But it does not seem that Hittite dominance ever extended farther eastwards than the land of the Hurrians and the region of the modern Sivas and Erzinjan, then called Azzi and Hayasa—the latter name being connected with the ancestors of the modern Armenians, who call themselves Haik. However, trade rela/ tions with the tribes and clans inhabiting Georgia were close, as witnessed by many affinities in technology and arts and crafts. Hittite and kindred cult influences made themselves strongly felt in Georgia. A classic instance of Anatolian cult penetration of Georgia is provided by a silver goblet from the Trialeti *kurgans*, which has a frieze depicting a procession of masked hierophants in attendance on a high priest enthroned between an enormous goblet/shaped vessel and a sacred tree, possibly a cedar. It may well be that we have here a representa/ tion of a Hittite fertility cult, and that the high priest and his acolytes are preparing some magic potion of immortality. The name of the Hittite god Telipinu springs to mind in this con/ nexion, particularly since the Svans of mountain Georgia also revere a folk deity with a somewhat similar name, Tulepia/ Melia or 'Tulepia the Fox'. Nor can we rule out some link with the Hittite feast of the Antahshum plant, celebrated in the spring to mark the rebirth of the vegetable world. The parallels between the Anatolian and Hittite pantheons and the ancient gods of the Georgian people have already been subjected to critical study by A. A. Zakharov, the late Mikheil Tsereteli and others, and there is little doubt that fresh discoveries will eventually supplement the sparse evidence at present at our disposal.

Plate 11

Chapter III

Tribes, Myths and Traveller's Tales

B ETWEEN 1200 AND 1190 BC, the Hittite empire finally collapsed in ruin under the impact of the 'Sea Peoples' who sailed in and surged inland from the Aegean and Mediter-ranean shores of Asia Minor. The unity of the Anatolian cul-ture pattern was once more violently disrupted. New tribal groups make their appearance at different points, and then vanish into obscurity or merge into larger and more lasting federations, such as the Phrygian kingdom and the Vannic kingdom of Urartu. The remains of the ancient Anatolian peoples, already subjugated for almost a millennium by the Hittites and related bearers of the Indo-European *kurgan* culture from the Eurasian steppes and partially absorbed by them, now found themselves under renewed pressure. Harried by the 'Sea Peoples' from the West, they were now confronted by the virile and aggressive Semitic empire of Assyria to the South. Thus it was that survivors of certain pre-Hittite peoples of Asia Minor found themselves pressed eastwards and northwards from the central Anatolian plateau into the mountainous Caucasian isthmus, where they could displace or merge with existing autochthonous elements and find a refuge from their predatory foes. From the chaotic maelstrom of the post-Hittite period in Asia Minor and Transcaucasia there eventually emerged the ethnic conglomerations and tribal groupings which were to form the nucleus of the modern Georgian and Armen-ian nations.

Fig. 10

It is during the years immediately following the fall of the Hittite empire that the historical records of Assyria begin to provide concrete data about the rulers and tribes who can be identified with some confidence as forerunners of the Georgians. It seems that various Caucasian and eastern Anatolian peoples

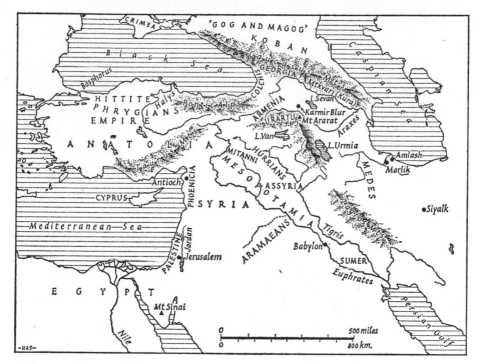

Fig. 10. Georgia in the Ancient World

who had been kept in check by the Hittites immediately took advantage of their collapse to swarm south-westwards into upper Mesopotamia and central Anatolia, thus coming into conflict with the kings of Assyria. Prominent among these intruders were the Gasgas or Kashki, a semi-barbarous people from the southern shores of the Black Sea, composed largely of swineherds, weavers and guerilla fighters, against whom the Hittite kings had been forced to send almost yearly expeditions; also a related people, the Mushki, who availed themselves of the disappearance of Hittite power to settle in the upper Euphrates region along the river Murad-su, in the districts of Alzi and Purulumzi. The Mushki entrenched themselves in this area around 1165 BC; some sixty-five years later, they were attacked and dispersed by King Tiglath-pileser I (1115–1077 BC), the Assyrians defeating five Mushki kings with 20,000 men. Following this reverse, the Mushki apparently split up, one branch proceeding westwards and settling in the southern reaches of the River Halys, where they mingled with the Phrygians to form an important kingdom; other Mushki retreated north-eastwards into Transcaucasia and settled in south-western Georgia, to form the nucleus of the prominent Georgian tribe of the Meskhians (the Moskhoi of the Greek geographers), whose province, Samtskhe, retains its distinctive identity up to the present day.

The Western Mushki had their moments of glory under King Mita (Midas), before Sargon of Assyria (722–705 BC) reduced the Mushki to submission. This King Mita was an ally of Kings Ambaris of Tabal and Rusa I of Urartu; he is now recognized as being identical with the famous Midas of the golden touch of Greek legend, who perished in 696/695 BC when his empire was destroyed by the Cimmerians. Under the name of Meshech, the Mushki are numbered in Biblical tradition among the sons of Japhet (*Gen.* x. 2; *1 Chron.* i. 5), and are associated with Tubal (Tabal) and Gomer (the Cimmerians), and also with Javan, that is to say, the Ionians or Greeks. Ezechiel (xxvii. 13) knew them as merchants, slave traders and metallurgists: 'Javan, Tubal and Meshech, they were thy merchants: they traded the persons of men and vessels of brass in thy market.' The same prophet (xxxii. 26) celebrates their ancient renown as pagan warriors in the highlands of Asia Minor: 'There is Meshech, Tubal, and all her multitude: her graves are round about him: all of them uncircumcised, slain by the sword, though they caused their terror in the land of the living.' Again Ezechiel cries (xxxviii. 1–4):

And the word of the Lord came unto me, saying,
Son of man, set thy face against Gog, the land of Magog,

the chief prince of Meshech and Tubal, and prophesy against him,

And say, Thus saith the Lord God: behold, I am against thee, O Gog, the chief prince of Meshech and Tubal:

And I will turn thee back, and put hooks into thy jaws, and I will bring thee forth, and all thine army horses and horsemen, all of them clothed with all sorts of armour, even a great company with bucklers and shields, all of them handling swords.

The people of Tubal, here associated with the Mushki, also have a lengthy history in the annals of Assyria. King Salmanesar III (859–824 BC) claims to have received tribute from the '24 kings of Tabal'. There is little doubt that Tabal (Tubal) also played a role in the process of ethnic mingling which resulted in the formation of the Georgian nation. Identified with the Tubal-cain of Genesis, famed as pioneer blacksmiths, this people crops up again in Classical times under the name Tibareni, this time on the south-western marches of Georgia. There exists a hypothesis, too complicated to discuss here, that the root *Tibar* gives rise to the form *Iber*, enabling us to account for the name—Iberoi or Iberians of the Caucasus—under which the Eastern Georgians were generally known throughout Classical and Byzantine times. This name was not used by the Georgians themselves, who call their land *Sakartvelo*, or 'country of the Kartvel people'.

Another important ethnic element on the borders of Anatolia and Caucasia was the confederation of the Daiaeni (Daiani) of the Assyrian sources, known to the Urartians as Diauehi (Diauhi), and as Taokhoi to the Greeks. Their importance lies in the fact that they gave their name to the mountainous south-western district of historical Georgia known to this day as Tao to the Georgians, or Taik to the Armenians (it is at present

within the eastern borders of Turkey), and also to the circum-
stance that they were the first political power on the territory
of Georgia whose kings are known to us by name. For example,
Tiglath-pileser I of Assyria in 1112 BC launched an attack on
the northern lands of Nairi, around lakes Van and Urmia, and
succeeded in capturing King Sieni of the Daiaeni, whom he
led back captive to his capital but eventually pardoned and
released. Considerably later, in 845 BC, King Salmanesar III
captured a king of Daiaeni, Asia by name, and then set him
free on condition that he offered the Assyrians tribute, including a gift of horses, and set up images of the Assyrian king in
his towns in token of allegiance. Around 790 BC the Diauehi
were in conflict with the Vannic kingdom of Urartu whose
king, Menua, captured Shashilu, royal city of the Diauehi, and
laid waste the country, with the result that the Diauehi king,
Utupurshini, appeared before Menua and sued for peace.

In fact, the Urartian inscriptions give extraordinarily accurate and detailed information about the population and mineral
and agricultural wealth of south-western Georgia during the
eighth and seventh centuries BC. They record, for instance, how
in 789 BC, King Argishti of Urartu won further victories over
the Diauehi, capturing 28,519 prisoners, plus 4426 horses,
10,478 head of cattle and 73,770 goats and other smaller
domestic animals. The defeated Diauehi king was obliged to
hand over to the Urartians some 20 kilograms of gold, 18 of
silver, several thousand kilograms of bronze, a thousand
horses, three hundred head of cattle and several thousand
smaller beasts, and also undertake to pay an annual tribute of
gold, bronze, oxen, cows, sheep and fine steeds. From these
data we can conclude that on the territory of the Georgian
province of Tao there existed at this early time a well-developed
tribal kingdom, with citadels and townships where goldsmiths
and silversmiths functioned alongside workers in copper and
bronze, and possessing a prosperous cattle and sheep raising

rural economy. Sturdy fighters, the Diauehi were the ancestors of those same Taokhoi who put up such a desperate resistance to Xenophon and his Ten Thousand, hurling themselves and their families over the cliffs rather than submit to foreign invaders.

Immediately north-east of the highland abodes of the Diauehi lay a land famous in ancient history and mythology— Colchis. Situated at the eastern end of the Black Sea, the territory of Colchis embraced the valley of the River Rioni (Phasis) and the adjoining sub-tropical region of marshes, forests and wooded hills which later constituted the provinces of Mingrelia, Guria and Atchara, with part of Imereti. One of the most important elements in the modern Georgian nation, the Colchians were probably established in the Caucasus by the Middle Bronze Age. It is possible that a people called the Kilkhi, who lived by the 'Upper (?Black) Sea' and were temporarily subjugated by the Assyrian king Tiglath-pileser I in the twelfth century BC, were in fact Colchians. It is certainly Colchians who figure prominently under the name Qulha (probably pronounced Qolha) in the annals of the Urartian King Sarduri II (764–735 BC), as carved in stone on the cliff by Lake Van. Sarduri II undertook two campaigns against Colchis, the first in 750–748 BC, the second between 744 and 741 BC. Speaking of his first expedition, Sarduri records: 'I set out against the land of Qulha. By the might of the God Khaldi I led Khakhani, king of the land of Khushalkhi, into captivity, together with his people, whom I deported and settled in my own realm.' In King Sarduri's second campaign, the Urartians captured and burnt one of the royal cities of Colchis, Ildamusha, and led the inhabitants away captive. Sarduri further states that he had a special iron plaque made to commemorate his victory over the Colchians, and set up memorial inscriptions in prominent places in their townships. According to Professor G. A. Melikishvili, this is the only reference to iron in the Urartian inscriptions, providing a useful indication as to the development of iron metallurgy in ancient Colchis.

It will thus be seen that Assyrian and Urartian records give a fairly coherent picture of the tribal groupings and the agricultural and mineral resources of the southern borderlands of Georgia during the Later Bronze and the Early Iron Age. For the northern regions of Transcaucasia, close to the main Caucasus range and outside the Urartian sphere, the absence of written materials obliges us to rely on the findings of archaeology, combined with what can be gleaned from ancient lore such as the myth of Prometheus and the story of Medea and the Argonauts. Fortunately the archaeological material for the Later Bronze Age in Georgia is exceptionally rich and varied. It was already made known to science in the nineteenth century in the classic studies of Chantre, and then by Jacques de Morgan, Tallgren, Hančar and others. Magnificent bronze weapons and other articles from the so-called Koban-Colchian culture have long featured prominently in the Georgian State Museum in Tbilisi and other Soviet collections, and even in museums outside Russia, such as that of St Germain-en-Laye in France; fresh finds are constantly enriching our knowledge of civilization in Georgia at the close of the Bronze Age and the beginning of the Iron Age.

It is common in specialist literature to distinguish two main culture zones in Georgia and adjoining areas at this period: firstly the Koban-Colchian culture, embracing most of western Georgia and a portion of eastern Georgia as far as the River Aragvi, also the southern and northern slopes of the central section of the main Caucasian range, including modern Ossetia; secondly the material culture characteristic of the remainder of eastern and south-western Georgia, namely Kakheti, Javakheti, Meskheti and parts of Kartli, together with western Azerbaijan and northern Armenia, this culture being provisionally designated by Shalva Amiranashvili and others

Plate 13

Figs. 11–13

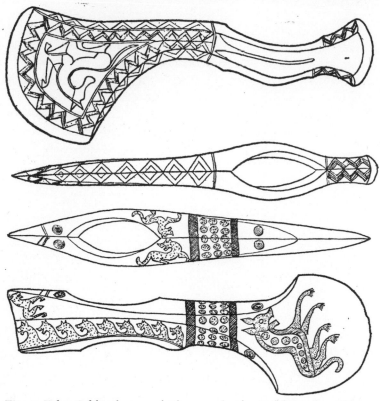

Fig. 11. Koban-Colchian bronze axeheads, engraved with animal figures, from Mekvena and Oni, western Georgia. 900 BC or later. Kutaisi Historical-Ethnographic Museum

Fig. 12. Koban-Colchian bronze axehead from Surmushi, showing swastika motif. 900 BC or later. Kutaisi Historical-Ethnographic Museum

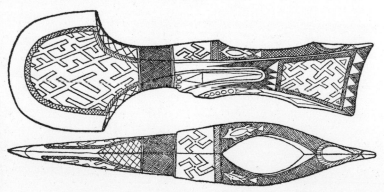

Fig. 13. Koban-Colchian bronze axehead from Oni. 900 BC or later. State Museum of Georgia, Tbilisi.
Such axeheads (see also Figs. 11, 12) are about 17 cm. long

as the 'Ibero-Meskho-Albanian culture'. Some authorities, including the Great Soviet Encyclopedia, regard the Colchian and Koban cultures as separate and distinct. The term Koban, incidentally, has nothing to do with the River Kuban, which flows through northern Caucasia, but relates to the burial ground at the village of Koban in northern Ossetia, where important and numerous finds of bronze objects were made from 1869 onwards. Within these Late Bronze Caucasian culture zones, various local sub-cultures may be distinguished, as for example the 'Bronze dagger sub-culture of Kakheti' defined and described by K. N. Pitskhelauri in 1959.

Fig. 14. Bronze belt showing hunting scene, from the Chabarukhi hoard, c. 1500 BC. Length about 90 cm. State Museum of Georgia, Tbilisi

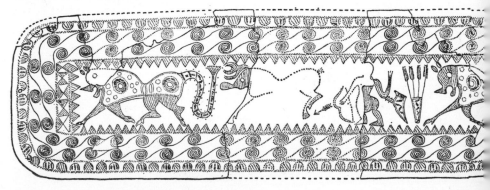

Among the distinctive features of the Koban-Colchian culture, which reached its peak between 900 and 800 BC, we may
single out a characteristic type of bronze axehead of elegant
form, often traced with stylized patterns depicting fantastic
animal figures. Along with this, at a somewhat later date, goes
a particular type of rectangular bronze belt buckle, in the centre
of which is a stylized animal figure. This beast is commonly
shown with head turned backwards, front legs bent, the back
part of the body raised up and the stomach arched. It is sometimes argued that this beast represents a wolf-totem and is connected with the ancient beliefs of the Caucasian mountaineers.
Certainly these Koban-Colchian animal figures, which coin-
cide with the first Scythian invasions of the Caucasus, exer-
cised a profound effect on the evolution of the famous 'Scythian animal style'. The artistic level of the metalwork of the
Ibero-Meskho-Albanian culture is also high. Examples of this
are found in the unusual broad girdles of thin bronze, decorated with hunting scenes and similar motifs, and discovered at
Samtavro close to Mtskheta and elsewhere. Significant also for
study of the life and beliefs of the ancient Caucasian tribes are
the curious ithyphallic figures discovered at Kazbek (Stepandsminda) on the Georgian Military Highway in 1877 by
G. D. Filimonov and frequently discussed by later archaeologists

Plate 12

Plates 19, 20

Plate 18
Fig. 14

Plate 17

and anthropologists. Imitations of such statuettes were apparently fabricated at Tbilisi as curios for sale to collectors. However, many examples are unmistakably authentic, and continue to come to light in various parts of Georgia as far east as central Kakheti, where they have been associated with finds of characteristic bronze daggers of the specific 'Kakhetian type', dated to between the thirteenth and eighth centuries BC. Some of these figurines were designed to be hung from drinking horns. They may be connected with the erotic and orgiastic cults and festivals such as the 'Berikoba' and 'Murqvamoba'—regularly celebrated until recent times among the Pshavs, Khevsurs, Svans and other Georgian mountaineer tribes, and with the cult of the fertility god Kviria.

Colchis and the Caucasus mountains were already familiar to the Greeks in the Homeric age. Of the Greek myths associated with Georgia and the Caucasus the best known are the legend of Prometheus, chained to Mount Elbruz by the jealous gods, and that of Jason and his band of Argonauts, their voyage in quest of the Golden Fleece, and the tragedy of the Colchian princess and enchantress Medea. In its legendary form, the story of the Golden Fleece reflects historical and economic reality, namely the quest by Greek merchant adventurers from Miletus for mineral wealth in the Caucasian region. From the seventh century BC, Greek colonists built up settlements and trading stations all round the eastern end of the Black Sea, among them Trapezus (Trebizond), Bathys (Batumi), Phasis (Poti), Dioscurias (Sukhumi) and Pitiunt (Pitsunda). The historical basis of the Argonaut legend was clear to the ancient geographers themselves, notably the shrewd Strabo (64 BC–AD 21), whose great-uncle Moaphernes had actually been administrator of Colchis under Mithradates Eupator, king of Pontus. Discussing the Argonaut legend, Strabo wrote that 'the city of Aea is still shown on the Phasis, and Aeëtes is believed to have ruled over Colchis, and the name Aeëtes is

Plate 8

still locally current among the people of that region. Again, Medea the sorceress is a historical person and the wealth of the regions about Colchis, which is derived from the mines of gold, silver, iron and copper, suggests a reasonable motive for the expedition.' (*Geog.*, trans. H. L. Jones, I. 2, para. 39.) Attempts have even been made to account for the Golden Fleece itself in terms of primitive prospecting techniques as employed in the Caucasus, as well as by the Forty-niners in the California Gold Rush. 'It is said,' Strabo reported (*Geog.* XI. 2, para. 19) 'that in their country gold is carried down by the mountain torrents, and that the barbarians obtain it by means of perforated troughs and fleecy skins, and that this is the origin of the myth of the Golden Fleece.' However this may be, the Argonaut legend is extremely ancient, evidently ante-dating the actual establishment of the Miletian colonies in Colchis. This is shown, as Dr Moses Hadas points out, by the passage in the *Odyssey* where Odysseus speaks of his trip through the Symplegades (*Odyssey*, XII. 70):

> Sole this voyage hath made, of the ships which fare on the
> ocean,
> Argo ever renowned, as she sailed from the land of Aeëtes.
> Aye and the Argo too on the huge rocks surely had driven
> Save for the guidance of Hera, who showed such favour to
> Jason.

The classic treatment of the Argonaut story, composed in verse by Apollonius Rhodius in the third century BC, consti-tutes a veritable gazetteer of the ports and tribes along the southern coast of the Black Sea, from Sinope eastwards to the River Phasis (Rioni). Though containing data culled from Xenophon's *Anabasis* and travellers' tales of lesser reliability, the work of Apollonius is valuable as a summary of the ideas of an educated Greek on the Colchians and their proto-Georgian neighbours. It is remarkable how many details in the

Argonautica corroborate the findings of archaeology, as well as the scattered references in the Hittite, Assyrian and Urartian sources. Between Sinope and Trebizond, for instance, the Argonauts encounter the semi-legendary iron-working tribe of the Chalybes, who 'take no thought for ploughing with oxen, nor for any planting of luscious fruit'.—'But cleaving open the stubborn earth with her store of iron, they do take therefrom a wage to barter for food; for them dawn never riseth without toil, but mid soot and flame and smoke they endure their heavy labour.' (*Argonautica*, trans. Edward P. Coleridge, p. 127.) The word *khalyps*, of course, means steel in Greek, and some scholars, such as Xavier de Planhol, doubt whether the Chalybes were an actual ethnic unit at all and regard the name as an epithet applied by the Greeks indiscriminately to all or any of the iron-working tribes of ancient Anatolia. Iron smelting evidently began in Asia Minor around 1400 BC, and the finished product was exported thence to Babylonia. There is a famous letter written around 1275 BC by the Hittite king Hattusilis III to one of his contemporaries, probably the king of Assyria, announcing the despatch of an iron dagger blade as a special gift. The Hittite iron-smelting centre was at a place called Kizzuwatna, which earlier scholars located in Pontus, in the home of the Chalybes. However, we now know that Kizzuwatna was in the south, embracing part of Cilicia. It seems likely that the Chalybes assumed pre-eminence in iron-forging at a somewhat later stage; they were renowned in their craft by the time of Herodotus and most of the other ancient geographers contain references to their specialized expertise. If they were not themselves of proto-Georgian stock, they were certainly of related Anatolian ancestry.

Further eastwards the Argonauts encounter other tribes evidently belonging to the Laz or Chan family of the Ibero-Caucasian people: the Tibareni, usually connected with Tabal/Tubal of the Old Testament, and then the quaint Mossynoeci, so called, it was said, because they lived in *mossynes*—wooden shelters and towers. Of the Tibareni the Greeks related that when the women entered childbirth, "'tis the men that throw themselves upon the beds and groan, with their heads veiled, while the women tend them carefully with food, and get ready for them the bath they use after child-birth'. (This curious custom, which anthropologists term *couvade*, is recorded among tribes in various parts of the world, including the Ainu of Hokkaido in northern Japan.) The Mossynoeci were depicted as immodest, tattooed barbarians, stuffing their young with chestnuts and copulating publicly in the middle of the street. Some of these allusions in the *Argonautica* stem from Herodotus and Xenophon and are exaggerated in the way of tall stories the world over. None the less, houses resembling the wooden structures of the Mossynoeci can be seen in Lazistan to this day. It is also interesting to note that the Mossynoeci are credited by pseudo-Aristotle with the discovery of brass which they produced, according to R. J. Forbes, by the cementation of copper with calamine. What is more, Xenophon's account of the poison honey found in the densely overgrown hinterland exactly matches reality. Modern travellers, including Denis Cecil Hills, have found that this toxic honey, collected by bees from bushes of *rhododendron flavum*, when eaten by human beings, actually produces the alarming symptoms described.

Quitting the shores of the Mossynoeci, the Argonauts sail on eastwards towards Colchis. Finally they arrive at the estuary of the River Phasis, almost within sight of their goal. In early times, the Greeks apparently gave the name Phasis to the modern River Chorokhi, which flows into the Black Sea not far south of Batumi, and only later transferred it to the modern Rioni, whose estuary is some 40 miles further north. At all events, it is worth noting that the Phasis gave its name to the 'Phasian bird' or pheasant—'Phasianus colchicus', as it is known to science. This bird is the type of the family *Phasianidae*, and is reared in England for shooting; it is distributed in its wild state from the Caspian Sea all over south-east Europe. The legend was that Jason and the Argonauts brought the bird back from Colchis and introduced it into Greece and the West.

At this point Apollonius Rhodius makes effective use of yet another Caucasian myth—that of Prometheus, whom Jason and his crew descry bound with bands of brass to the steep cliffs of Mount Elbruz, a prey to the eagle who swooped down each evening to feast on the captive titan's liver.

On arrival at the Phasis estuary, the Argonauts furl their sails and take to their oars, rowing upstream with the lofty Caucasus upon their left hand, until they reach 'the Cytaean town of Aea'—the modern Kutaisi—and the plain of Ares and that god's hallowed grove, where the serpent guarded the Golden Fleece as it hung on the branches of the sacred oak.

The remaining episodes of the saga—the sowing of the dragon's teeth, the guilty passion of Medea for Jason, the theft of the Fleece, the murder of Absyrtus and the retribution of the gods—are too well known to need repeating here. Noteworthy, however, is the description given by Apollonius Rhodius of the ancient, pre-Hellenic Colchian kingdom, a picture drawn centuries after the era reflected in the legend, but reproducing faithfully the lore about the Caucasus as known to the ancient world. There is a description of the alleged burial customs of the Colchians, who wrapped the bodies of their men in untanned hides and suspended them from trees well away from human habitation; the corpses of females, on the other hand, were consigned to the ground. Apollonius recreates vividly the aspect of the palace and gardens of King Aeëtes at Cytaean Plate 8   Aea—'fenced walls and wide gates and columns, which stood in rows upholding the walls; and above the house was a coping of stone resting upon triglyphs of bronze . . . And nigh thereto were garden-vines in full blossom, shooting on high, and

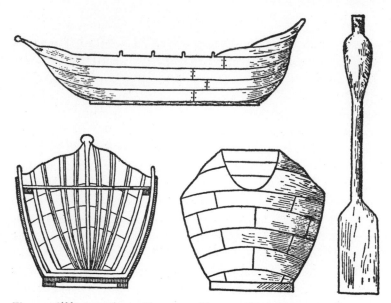

Fig. 15. Abkhazian eight-oared boat, as used by Heniochi pirates in antiquity

covered with green young foliage ...' (*Argonautica*, trans. Coleridge, p. 155.) Thanks to the excavations of B. A. Kuftin, we now have some conception of ancient Colchian architecture, while archaeologists have unearthed many traces of ancient viticulture throughout Georgia, including the Rioni valley in which Aea was situated. Other facts about King Aeëtes and his subjects given in the *Argonautica*—for instance, the numerous and warlike Colchian army and well-equipped fleet—are corroborated by the annals of Urartu, whose land forces were often deployed against Qulha, and by later Greek sources which allude to the marauding activities of the Heniochi, pirates living further up the Black Sea coast, and to the important contribution of the Colchians to the fleet of King Mithradates Eupator of Pontus. *Fig. 15*

Like the legend of the Golden Fleece, the Prometheus myth also has its roots in pre-Homeric times and is connected with ancient mining and metallurgy. Several of the Caucasian peoples, including the Georgians, the Kabardians, the Abkhazians and the Ossetes, have their own indigenous version of the story. In the Georgian recensions, the rebellious titan is given the name Amiran. Some scholars think that the Prometheus legend is in fact a product of the national traditions of the Caucasian peoples, who passed it on to Greek settlers, while themselves handing it down locally through the ages by the medium of the village story-teller; others take the view that the Georgians, having close ties with Hellenistic and Byzantine culture, had ample opportunity to read Aeschylus and other Greek books, from which the tale of Prometheus could have passed into the realm of Georgian popular culture. It is interesting to note that the adversary of Amiran, the Georgian 'Prometheus', is not Zeus, but Jesus Christ. Son of a Caucasian sorcerer, Amiran is a loud-mouthed braggart, who murders Christians and then engages Jesus Christ in a rock-throwing contest in which both hurl vast boulders and crags miles up into the heavens. Christ's rock embeds itself deep into the earth, and He challenges Amiran to pull it out. Amiran fails, and is chained to that same rock. 'Christ gave him one loaf of bread every day, and a little dog for company. That little dog licks and licks at the chain, and by his licking he keeps on wearing the chain away—to such an extent that with a few licks more, Amiran will burst it apart and free himself. But on the Thursday morning before Easter the blacksmiths arise and strike away with their hammers, so that the chain is made solid again. Oh, if Amiran ever manages to burst the chain apart! What a terrible fate would then befall the blacksmiths—he will knock the heads off every one of them.'

Another important version of the Prometheus legend is current among the Abkhazians, successors of the ancient pirate people of the Heniochi, whose territory bordered on Colchis. The hero, Abrskil by name, is pictured in some variants as the national hero of Abkhazia, waging war against evil in the interests of his people; in others, he appears as an arrogant and destructive giant, with a mania for killing all persons with fair hair and blue eyes, on the ground that they are possessed of the Evil Eye. One typical version depicts Abrskil as a friend of the human race, who communicates to mankind the secrets of the heavens, as did Prometheus. When bracken and clinging jungle lianas choke the crops, Abrskil clears the ground for men to cultivate. Abrskil's superhuman prowess and services to mankind arouse the jealousy of Almighty God, who commands angels to chain him up in a cavern. A black hound gnaws away at the chain, but when the links become as thin as a thread, a maiden sitting on guard notifies an evil witch, who reinforces the chain once more with her magic wand. If some bold mortal ventures into Abrskil's murky cavern, the titan will cry out: 'Turn back! Only tell me first, do bracken and weeds still grow upon the earth? Are there still brambles and thorn bushes? Do wicked men still oppress the weak?'— 'Yes', the visitor sadly replies.—The chain rattles and the hero groans: 'Alas, not yet does happiness reign in my native land, no peace is there yet for man upon the earth.'

CHAPTER IV

Caucasian Iberia and Colchis
in Classical Times

TOWARDS THE END of the eighth century BC, Trans, caucasia and Anatolia underwent a series of barbarian invasions, the devastating effects of which were comparable with those of the Indo,European onslaught which broke up the Anatolian Chalcolithic and Early Bronze Age culture around 2100 BC and those of the arrival of the Sea Peoples who destroyed the Hittite Empire about 1200 BC. This time the invaders were Cimmerians and Scythians from the north Caucasian steppe,lands. About 730 BC hordes of Cimmerians descended on Colchis from the direction of the Sea of Azov, skirting the Black Sea coast, to be followed shortly afterwards by waves of Scythians surging over the Daryal Pass close to Mount Kazbek in the central Caucasus and along the western shore of the Caspian Sea, past Derbent and the site of modern Baku. Besides the eloquent account of Herodotus, the presence of large numbers of Scythians and Cimmerians in Georgia is attested by Scythian burials and finds of Scythian arrowheads and other characteristic items at the Samtavro burial ground at Mtskheta, also in Trialeti, in Abkhazia and elsewhere. Trialeti had been a great centre for the *kurgan* peoples who had arrived, also from northern Caucasia, more than a millennium earlier; now it was settled by a tribe of Cimmerians called 'Treri' (in Armenian, 'Trel')—hence, perhaps, the region's modern name Trial,eti, which in Georgian means 'land of the Trial'. The Scythians and Cimmerians assimilated many of the tech, niques of Caucasian metallurgy, including elements of the famous Caucasian 'animal style', and other advanced local forms of technology and methods of agriculture.

Fig. 16

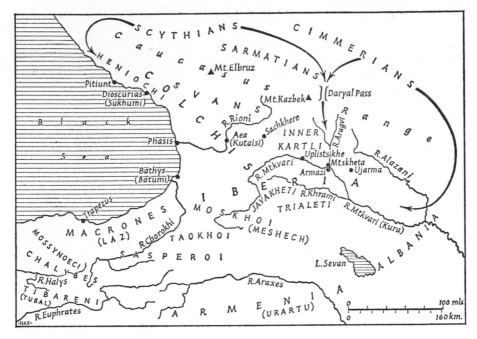

Fig. 16. Colchis and Iberia

From their new bases in Georgia, the Scythians and Cimmerians fanned out to the west, south and south-east. They invaded Media, ravaged the Phrygo-Mushkian kingdom of King Midas and plundered the Greek colony of Sinope. They stormed into Syria and Palestine and even approached the borders of Egypt, bringing terror to the people of Israel, as attested by the references to Gomer (the Cimmerians) and Gog and Magog (in this instance, the Scythians) in the writings of the prophet Ezechiel. They prepared the way for the downfall of both Assyria and Urartu, the latter kingdom being finally overthrown and in part incorporated into the empire of the Medes around 590 BC.

This cataclysm had far-reaching effects on the kingdom of Colchis and the various Ibero-Caucasian and kindred tribes

73

living in north-eastern Anatolia and Georgia proper. The old tribal federations of the Mushki, the Diauehi and the Col- chians were severely dislocated. Many of these Ibero-Caucasian tribes, ancestors of the Georgians of today, took to the hills or became vassals of the Medes and Persians. Under Darius and Xerxes, during the heyday of the Achaemenid empire, Hero- dotus notes that the Sasperoi, Alarodians, Moskhoi, Tibareni, Mossynoeci and related peoples formed part of the 18th and 19th satrapies of the Persian state, to which they furnished annual tribute totalling five hundred talents of silver. When describing the motley array of Xerxes' army, Herodotus (VII. 78-9) brings the Moskhoi on parade with wooden helmets on their heads and carrying shields and small spears with long points. The Tibareni, Macrones and Mossynoeci were equipped in the same way, while the Colchians were armed with swords and shields of raw oxhide. Every five years, the Colchians sent a 'voluntary' tribute of one hundred boy slaves and one hun- dred girls to the Persian king-of-kings.

Within a century, by 400 BC, the power of the Achaemenid empire waned greatly as a result of dynastic feuds and the resur- gence of Hellas. When Xenophon and his Ten Thousand crossed Transcaucasia and the Pontic Alps, he found that the proto-Georgian tribes had reasserted their independence of the Persians. However, these tribes and clans were now under pressure from another source, namely the new and growing might of the Armenian nation, rapidly developing into one of the important powers of the East. The origins of the Armenians remain somewhat obscure; though their language is classed as Indo-European, it has a Caucasian sub-stratum, and their ethnic make-up is compounded of many elements derived from ancient Anatolian peoples, in particular the Hurrians and other inhabitants of Urartu. Between the seventh and second cen- turies BC, the Armenians established themselves as the successor state to Urartu, whose ancient territory they took over and

greatly extended in various directions. This Armenian expan-
sion inevitably affected the Ibero-Caucasian tribes, who found
themselves pushed back still further northwards on the Black
Sea littoral and north-eastwards up into the Caucasus mountains. North of Lake Van, troglodytic Armenians had by
Xenophon's time largely supplanted the old Diauehi of Urartian days. Strabo (*Geog.* XI. 41, para. 5) later mentions how
the Iberians or Eastern Georgians lost vast tracts of land in the
upper Mtkvari valley, notably the province of Gogarene, while
the Chalybes and Mossynoeci were deprived of much of their
ancient habitat south of Trebizond, these lost territories being
annexed to the new Armenian kingdom.

Pressure from the south contributed, together with various
political, social and economic factors, to accelerate and intensify
the unification of the scattered Ibero-Caucasian tribes and
principalities into three larger socio-political entities. These
entities in their turn corresponded more or less closely to the
linguistic breakdown of the Kartvelian peoples, persisting to
this day, into Georgian, Svanian and Mingrelo-Laz speakers,
as well as subsidiary dialects of each of them. The Mingrelo-
Laz speakers comprised the bulk of the ancient Colchian
population of the Phasis (Rioni) valley, together with the
remaining hill tribes inhabiting the Pontic Alps region between
Batumi and Trebizond. The Svans occupied remote fastnesses
immediately south of Mount Elbruz in the main Caucasian
chain, comprising the modern districts of Svaneti, Ratcha and
Lechkhumi and also other districts of Imereti or western
Georgia. The Georgians proper, the Iberians of antiquity, came
to statehood rather later than their Colchian cousins; their land
came to include all of eastern Georgia, including Kartli, the
district round the modern capital of Tbilisi (Tiflis), Kakheti,
Samtskhe, Trialeti, Javakheti and Tao-Klarjeti. As already
mentioned, it is sometimes argued that the Greek name
for the eastern Georgians—'Iberoi'—derives either from the

palaeo-Caucasian nation of the Tibareni (Tubal/Tabal of the Assyrians) or else from that of the Sasperoi of the Ispir region on the River Chorokh. At all events, the Classical Iberian kingdom, unified by a common, Georgian tongue, came to include a number of important and ancient ethnic groups, including the remains of the Diauehi (Taokhoi), the Moskhoi (Meskhians), remnants of the Urartian kingdom, Scythian immigrant groups from North Caucasia, together with autoch-thonous elements whose forbears had lived in Transcaucasia probably for several millennia.

As with the Armenians, it was the development and adop-tion of a common language and common forms of religion and state organization that enabled the Georgians to survive cor-porately into modern times, and to build up over the centuries an important political organism and a durable literature and culture. Linguistic unification was vital, in view of the tre-mendous ethnic diversity of the Caucasian region, which per-sists to this day. Two thousand years ago, Strabo was already commenting on the fact that seventy different tribes used to mingle in the markets of Dioscurias, the modern Sukhumi, on the Black Sea coast above Colchis—'though others, who care nothing for the facts, actually say three hundred' (*Geog.* XI. 2, para. 16)—'All speak different languages because of the fact that, by reason of their obstinacy and ferocity, they live in scattered groups and without intercourse with one another.' Apart from the Georgians, not one of these seventy Caucasian peoples possessed a written language of their own until modern Russian colonizers provided some of them with alphabets in

Plate 29

the nineteenth and twentieth centuries. The Georgians and Colchians on the other hand long had an excellent command of Greek and Iranian (Armazic) writing, and from the fifth century AD evolved a scientifically precise alphabet of their own, which is entirely different from the Cyrillic and remains in use today under the Soviet regime.

The origins of the Georgian, as of other Caucasian languages, remain controversial. Marr's grandiose Japhetic theory (see p. 24) has long been in ruins, though some excellent scholars believe that Georgian, Basque, and certain north Caucasian languages share a common ancestry. Others postulate a 'proto⁄Caucasian' language, from which the Kartvelian, Adyghe⁄Circassian, Checheno⁄Ingush and Daghestanian languages would all trace descent. Only the filiation of the Kartvelian (Ibero⁄Caucasian) languages with one another seems relatively clear, and may be summarized in the following pedigree, which is based on the work of the late Professor Gerhard Deeters:

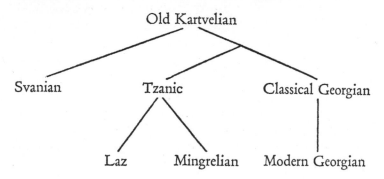

Laz and Mingrelian are subdivisions of the ancient Col⁄chian or Tzanic tongue, once spoken extensively all round the eastern end of the Black Sea. In early medieval times, from the seventh century AD, Georgian speakers from the East crossed the Surami range and Lesser Caucasus into Colchis and drove a wedge through to the Black Sea, via the modern Guria and Atchara. As a result, the Laz and Mingrelians lost touch with one another and their respective languages developed along separate lines. Opinions differ as to when the original old Kartvelian split into its present⁄day components. Using the modern technique known as glottochronology, a Soviet lin⁄guist, G. A. Klimov, would make Georgian and Tzanic evolve jointly from Old Kartvelian around the nineteenth century BC, during Georgia's Early Bronze Age, and then split apart from one another about the eighth century BC, during the early Caucasian Iron Age. Georgian and Tzanic exhibit greater resemblance to one another than either do to Svanian, making it probable, if we accept this reconstruction, that Svanian split off directly from Old Kartvelian in the second millennium BC. This would fit with the account of Strabo, who describes the Svans as a separate nation, long entrenched in the Caucasian highlands well away from other speakers of the Ibero-Caucasian languages. All this is somewhat hypo-thetical; yet it is relevant to take into account the great antiquity of the indigenous Georgian place names. Towns such as Kutaisi (Cytaean Aea), Shorapani (Sarapana), Tsitsamuri (Sevsamora) and Harmozika (Armaz-tsikhe), and rivers such as the Aragvi and Alazani are already known to the ancient Greeks by their local Georgian names or by close approxima-tions to them. Many of these outlandish names, even when given in Greek transcription, are clearly of local, Georgian origin; they can readily be distinguished from descriptive titles like 'Rhodopolis' or 'Archaeopolis', or nicknames like 'wooden-house dwellers' or 'lice-eaters' which the Greeks themselves bestowed on certain Caucasian places and tribes. The study of Georgian and Caucasian toponymics reinforces the conviction that substantial elements of the modern Georgian nation were autochthonous, or at least settled in Caucasia at a very remote period.

The evolution of more advanced forms of government and social organization in Georgia and adjoining regions was fostered during the last centuries before Christ by rapid im-provements in agriculture and technology. Iron ploughs and other implements came into use. All branches of metallurgy made progress. Throughout the Black Sea region, Georgian timber was in demand for boat building. Agricultural methods

Fig. 17

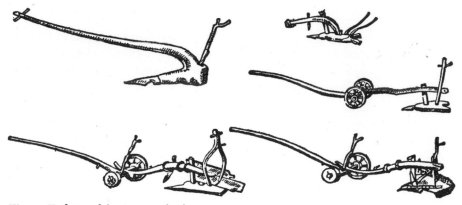

Fig. 17. Evolution of the Georgian plough

evolved and the area of land under cultivation increased, land utilization being fostered by drainage and irrigation schemes. Vine-growing and wine-making became an important indus- try. Storage of home-made wine in large clay pots or *pithoi* (Georgian: *kvevri*), buried in the earth, was widely practised, and is still universal in Georgia to this day. Urn burial was common, and the urns used were usually worn-out wine storage jars. This is attested by archaeologists, who scrape from inside such burial urns bits of grape skin and pips remaining from wine drunk more than two thousand years ago. M. M. Ivashchenko discovered in western Georgia a number of skeletons interred in these clay urns, each having a silver coin inserted in its mouth to pay the fare across the River Styx into the Hereafter in Charon's ghostly ferry-boat.

Important for the social development of Georgia in Classical times was the integration of Colchis and Iberia into the inter- national trade route system. While seventy polygot tribes did business with the Greek settlers and Roman soldiers at Dios- curias, further south Phasis (the modern Poti) at the mouth of the Rioni was a busy port, whence ships made regular sailings

Plate 4

Plate 5

to Amisus and Sinope. Colchian linen was exported in bulk, also hemp, wax and pitch. The Greeks brought in fine pottery and vases, articles of luxury, jewellery and a wide range of manufactured goods. The prosperity of Colchis spread eastwards over the Surami range and along the Kura valley. The upper reaches of the Rioni, traversed by more than a hundred bridges, were guarded by an important fort at Sarapana, the modern Shorapani. From there, goods could be transported by waggon along the Kura valley to the Caspian Sea and transhipped over to Bactria, the entrepot for the Chinese silk trade and the Indian spice route. In return exotic wares from the Orient would pass westwards through Caucasian Albania and Iberia over to Colchis, for distribution in the markets of Greece and the Mediterranean world.

An attendant and highly significant phenomenon of this period was the progress of Colchis and adjoining regions of Caucasia from barter to a fully-fledged money economy, which took place from about 500 BC onwards. Using some of the enormous local deposits of Pontic silver, an abundant and varied silver coinage was minted, doubtless at Phasis and Dioscurias for the most part, and circulated intensively in western Georgia and occasionally in other Black Sea coastal areas as far afield as the Crimea, though rather seldom in Armenia and eastern Georgia (Iberia). The Colchian coinage is Hellenistic in style, though the weight standard is adapted to the Perso-Achaemenian monetary system. Denominations were hemidrachms, drachms, didrachms and, rarely, tetradrachms. The most common variety is the small silver hemidrachm showing

Plate 74b

on the obverse a female head, sometimes surmised to be that of Medea or the Georgian wood-goddess Dali, facing to the right; the reverse shows a bull's head, representing one of the main branches of the country's economy, cattle-breeding, unless we have here one of the fire-belching bulls of King Aeëtes. One unusual design, belonging this time to the larger didrachm,

features a crouching hermaphrodite lion, with a long mane and
prominent teats, and on the reverse, a kneeling human figure
with a bull's head, somewhat resembling the legendary minotaur. Following the great epoch of Alexander of Macedon,
whose conquests had far-reaching effects in Anatolia and
Transcaucasia, barbarous local imitations of gold staters of
Alexander and Lysimachus were manufactured and circulated
both in Colchis and in eastern Georgia. The Alexander
staters are more commonly found in eastern parts of Georgia,
the Lysimachus ones in Colchis and western, Black Sea areas
of the country. During the time of King Mithradates Eupator
of Pontus, around 100 BC, the city of Dioscurias (Sukhumi)
began issuing a local bronze coinage showing the caps of
Castor and Pollux, the Dioscuri, surmounted by six- or eight-
pointed stars. In Iberia or eastern Georgia, silver coins of the
Roman emperor Augustus later became common, as well as
those of the Parthian kings; crude local imitations of these
were made and circulated, the Roman denarii being in heavy
demand for paying local Roman garrison troops.

Plate 74a

Plate 74e

From the destruction of the old Colchian kingdom by the
Scythians up to the formation of the kingdom of Lazica in
Byzantine times, the Colchians, prosperous though they were,
failed to leave much of a mark on the political history of Caucasia. This was partly due to the pestilential, malarial climate
of the Rioni delta, with its unhealthy swamps. Writers such as
pseudo-Hippocrates allude in fact to the sallow, sickly and
flaccid appearance of the Colchians and their indolent temperament. At one time, they were ruled by provincial dynasts
known as *sceptukhs* or sceptre-bearers. Mithradates Eupator
(120–63 BC), the great king of Pontus and Rome's formidable
enemy in the East, brought Colchis under his sway and appointed his son, Prince Mithradates, to be viceroy. Soon afterwards this prince was charged with treason and put to death,
following which governors were set over Colchis, one of them

Plate 74d

Plates 31, 32

being Strabo's great-uncle Moaphernes. Pompey's invasion of Georgia in 66–65 BC brought both Colchis and Iberia into the Roman orbit. Pompey appointed a certain Aristarchus to be dynast of Colchis, as commemorated on silver coins struck in Aristarchus' name and depicting Pompey himself. Subsequently Colchis belonged to Polemo I, king of Pontus and then, until AD 23, to his widow Pythodoris. The Romans then divided Colchis into four small principalities and appointed rulers over them at their own discretion.

In these circumstances, political hegemony in Georgia naturally passed into the hands of the better organized and less vulnerable new kingdom of the Iberians, which developed in central and eastern Georgia during the last four centuries BC. The Iberian nation, we have seen, represented a consolidation of ancient ethnic groupings of the Transcaucasian region, together with the remains of the Diauehi (Taokhoi), the Moskhoi (Meskhians) and other Anatolian elements. To judge by the abundance of warrior graves of the period, the supremacy of the Iberians over the Scythians, Cimmerians and other Indo-European invaders of the Kura valley was not won without a struggle. The earliest cities of the Iberians were fortified strongholds like the troglodytic rock-town of Uplistsikhe near Gori. Later on, the political centre of Iberia moved eastwards down the river Kura to the vicinity of Mtskheta, a city whose name is sometimes explained as 'city of the Meskhians', though this etymology remains debatable. Situated at the confluence of the rivers Aragvi and Kura, Mtskheta-Armazi is the site of an enormous and ancient necropolis, that of Samtavro, and was defended by the two massive strongholds of Harmozika—Armaz-tsikhe, or 'castle of Ahura-Mazda'—situated on Mount Bagineti, and Sevsamora on the left bank of the Aragvi.

Possession of ancient Iberia was a prize worth fighting for. Its wealth is revealed by the amazing splendour of gems and precious metals consigned to the earth together with the corpses

of local princes and princesses, such as the so-called Akhalgori Plate 28
hoard of Achaemenid gold and precious objects discovered in
1908 in the Ksani valley and described in a special monograph by Ya. I. Smirnov (1934). The flourishing international
trade connexions with Persia and central Asia apart, Strabo
and other Greek and Roman authorities agree that whereas
most tribes of the Caucasus occupied 'barren and cramped territories', the eastern Georgians as well as the Albanians in
present-day Soviet Azerbaijan possessed 'territory that is fertile
and capable of affording an exceedingly good livelihood'
(*Geog.* XI. 2, para. 19)—statements which apply equally today.
The lowland farmers, we are told, lived and dressed rather like
the Medes and Armenians, while the fierce Georgian highlanders resembled the Scythians and Sarmatians, with whom
they maintained constant relations. By the beginning of the
Christian era the greater part of Iberia, as Strabo says, was well
built up where cities and farmsteads were concerned, their
houses, market places and public buildings being constructed
with architectural skill. These observations are amply borne
out by excavations carried out over the past thirty years by the
Georgian Academy of Sciences, and summarized in such distinguished publications as Dr Andria Apakidze's treatise on
Towns and Urban Life in ancient Georgia, and the Academy's
own detailed excavation report on the Mtskheta expedition,
the first volume of which appeared at Tbilisi in 1955.

The political organization and social structure of pre-
Christian Caucasian Iberia had much in common with contemporary Hellenizing kingdoms of Asia Minor and central
Asia during the Seleucid period. The Georgian Annals
(*Kartlis tskhovreba*, 'The Life of Georgia') give a picturesque,
legendary version of the beginnings of kingship in Iberia, con-
necting it with the name of Alexander the Great, who never
actually invaded Georgia at all, but is credited throughout the
East with all manner of buildings and mighty feats. According

to these Annals, Alexander entrusted the administration of Georgia to a relative of his by the name of Azon (very likely a confusion with the name Jason, of Argonaut fame), who proved such a tyrant as to alienate not only the Georgians, but even the Greeks whom he had brought with him. The oppressed Georgians revolted under the lead of Parnavaz, a descendant of Kartlos, eponymous ancestor of the Kartvelian or Georgian nation, after whom Sakartvelo, land of the Georgians, is named. This Parnavaz was a nephew of Samara, patriarch of the Iberians of Mtskheta; with the help of King Kuji of Colchis, Parnavaz drove out Azon and his Greek mercen- aries, and was recognized by the Kings of Syria and Armenia as legitimate ruler of Iberia. He reorganized the army of the Kartlosids and appointed seven or eight *eristavis* or 'heads of the people', one of whom was made *spaspet* or commander in chief. These officers were each assigned one province of Georgia to govern, the *spaspet* being responsible for the central area of Inner Kartli, around Mtskheta and Uplistsikhe. It seems that this office of *spaspet* was in fact occupied by the member of the

Fig. 18. Intaglio sardonyx ring bezel of the pitiakhsh *(governor) Asparukh of Iberia, c. AD 200. 2 × 2 × 1.8 cm. From Armazi*

Iberian royal family next in seniority to the king: Strabo states that in the royal hierarchy, 'the second in line administers justice and commands the army' (*Geog.* XI. 3, para. 6). It is possible also to equate these high dignitaries with the viceroys of Iberia whose hereditary necropolis was uncovered in Mtskheta-Armazi (see p. 82), together with engraved gems bearing portraits of two of them, Zevakh and Asparukh. These viceroys bore the Iranian title of *pitiakhsh* or *bdeashkh*, roughly approximating to that of satrap. Other official and court titles of which we have record include those of royal architect and *epitropos* or lord chamberlain, or master of the Court.

Plates 23–27

Fig. 18

According to Strabo, there existed four main castes or classes in Iberian society during the Classical period. These were the royal family; the priesthood; the free warriors and yeoman farmers; and 'the common people, who are slaves of the king and perform all the services that pertain to human livelihood'. The priests also acted as diplomats, in that they 'attended to all matters of controversy with the neighbouring peoples'. The slaves, many of them prisoners of war, looked after the needs of the royal household and aristocracy, and toiled at public works such as the building of the enormous ramparts at the castles at Mtskheta-Armazi, Uplistsikhe and other centres. We must, however, agree with Academician Ya. A. Manandyan that chattel slaves did not play a role in the economy of Classical Armenia and Georgia comparable to that played by slaves in Rome, Egypt or Greece, where they were organized and exploited on a broad industrial scale. Even at this early date, the trend was rather for Caucasian slaves to be kidnapped and sold into the larger markets of the Near East. The Heniochi, Strabo tells us (*Geog.* XI. 2. para. 12), would raid the wooded regions around Colchis, hide their portable boats in the forests and 'wander on foot night and day for the sake of kidnapping people', whom they held to ransom or sold into slavery. This trade later reached its climax in Ottoman times. We have little specific information about the existence of a Georgian merchant and artisan class in Classical times, probably because this was composed, then as later, largely of Greeks, Armenians, Jews, Persians and other foreign elements.

Unlike the more pliant Colchians, the Iberians of Eastern Georgia offered a desperate resistance to Pompey's invasion of 66–65 BC. King Artag and his warriors took refuge in trees, from which they rained arrows and missiles onto the Roman legionaries until the forests themselves were burnt or hacked down. Once Roman hegemony was established, however, the Iberians rapidly adapted themselves to Roman ways, which had far-reaching effects on Georgia's social and economic life. The building of roads gave the country access to markets in Asia Minor and other parts of the Roman Empire. The kings of Iberia became 'friends and allies of the Roman people', and went with their knights on several embassies to Rome, where they impressed the Emperor Hadrian by feats of horsemanship and agility. An inscription of Vespasian dating from AD 75 and discovered near Mtskheta shows that the Romans sent engineers there to build fortifications against the Scythians, Sarmatians and other marauders, and to reinforce the all-important route over the Caucasus through the Daryal Pass—

Fig. 19
Plate 30

'the gate of the Alans'. Roman baths, amphitheatres and other characteristic edifices now adorned Mtskheta-Armazi and the principal cities of the Iberian kingdom.

This did not mean, however, that the Iberians abandoned their ancient cultural links with Iran, ruled at this period by the Parthian dynasty of the Arsacids, sworn foes of the Romans. The virile dominion of the Arsacids lasted in Iran from 249 BC until the battle of Hormuz in AD 226, which opened the way for the rise of the empire of the Sasanids. Symptomatic of the mingled Iranian and Graeco-Roman influences in the life and customs of the Georgian upper classes are the names borne by the Iberian kings and high officials during the period. Along-

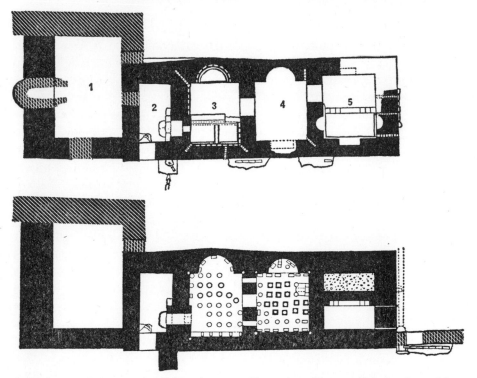

Fig. 19. Roman bath at Armazis-Khevi, close to Mtskheta. Plans of basement (below) and ground floor (above). Over-all length 21 m.: (1) Dressing room; (2) heating chamber; (3) hot bath; (4) warm bath; (5) cold bath

side Iranian names like Parnavaz, Farasmanes (Farsman), Ksefarnug and Asparukh, we encounter an impeccable Roman form like Publicius Agrippa, and even hybrid combinations such as Flavius Dades.

This eclectic, syncretizing tendency is apparent when we come to study the religious cults of ancient Iberia and Colchis. As direct descendants of ancient peoples of Anatolia, some of the tribes who helped to form the nucleus of the Iberian nation inherited cults and beliefs closely akin to those of the Hittites, Phrygians, perhaps even the Sumerians, Assyrians and

Plate 11

Babylonians. Testifying to this are the Trialeti goblet, with its scenes from a fertility rite connected with the Tree of Life and the potion of immortality, as well as the resemblances between certain orgiastic ceremonies of the Caucasian highlanders and ritual practices of Anatolian and Near Eastern antiquity. The Georgian national sources, namely the chronicle *Kartlis Tskhovreba* ('The Life of Georgia') and the Life of Saint Nino, contain picturesque though sometimes fanciful data about the official cults of pagan Georgia. According to Saint Nino's biographer, the Georgian national gods were named Armazi (to be identified with Ahura-Mazda of the Zoroastrian pan-theon), Zaden, Gatsi and Gaim. Armazi is depicted in the Life of Saint Nino as an idol in the form of a man made of copper, clothed in golden armour and having shoulder pieces and eyes made from emeralds and beryl stones, and holding in his hand a sword which revolved in his grasp. Gatsi was a golden idol, Gaim a silver one with a human face. These images were worshipped, says the pious hagiographer, by the royal court at Mtskheta-Armazi and all the common people. When Saint Nino offered up a prayer to God, the Almighty sent down hail 'in lumps as big as two fists' on to the abode of the heathen idols and smashed them into little pieces. This miracle unfortunately deprives us of the opportunity of judging for ourselves whether these Georgian sources really give a faith-ful account of the cults of pagan Georgia, or whether they are not somewhat embellished with reminiscences of Baal, Moloch and kindred deities of Old Testament fame. Simple folk whom Saint Nino encountered at the town of Urbnisi worshipped the sacred fire of the Zoroastrians, and also images of stone and wood; there was, too, a miracle-working tree to which the people attributed wondrous powers of healing. Tree worship is also attested in Georgia through the cult of the wood-goddess Dali, who corresponds to Artemis in Greek mythology. Byzantine accounts of the Emperor Justinian's Lazic wars speak of tree

Fig. 20. Horse standing before Mithraic fire-altar, engraved on the inside of a silver bowl from Armazi. Second century AD

worship as an official cult among the Abasgians (Abkhazians) of the Black Sea up to the sixth century AD.

The prevalence of Mazdaism in Georgia is confirmed by the archaeological evidence, which includes no less than five silver bowls discovered at Armazi and at a place called Bori, depicting the sacrificial figure of a horse standing before the ritual firealtar. One of the bowls even has an inscription in Middle Persian, commemorating a dignitary named 'Buzmihr the good *pitiakhsh*', the name being an abbreviated form of 'BuzurgMihr' or Mithra the Great. In Colchis, the gods and goddesses of the Greek pantheon were revered by members of the ruling classes who were in touch with the Hellenic cultural sphere of the Black Sea. Strabo (*Geog.* II, ii, para. 17) speaks of a temple of the sungoddess Leucothea and an oracle of Phrixus in the land of the Moskhoi—the Georgian province of Samtskhe; this temple was formerly rich but was later desecrated and robbed of its treasures. A temple of Apollo existed at Phasis (Poti) at the mouth of the Rioni as early as the fifth century BC, as witness the discovery in north Caucasia in 1901 of a silver drinking bowl of that period with the inscription: 'I belong to

Fig. 20

Apollo the Supreme of Phasis.' Later, a huge statue of the goddess Rhea also stood in a conspicuous site on the Phasis estuary. The people of the extreme eastern regions of Georgia, the modern Kakheti, shared with the Caucasian Albanians a cult of the sun and moon, Helios and Selene. An important moon temple was situated, according to Strabo, 'near Iberia', probably in the Alazani valley. The chief priest of the moon-goddess was held in high honour, having charge of extensive tracts of temple lands and also of the temple slaves, many of whom were 'subject to religious frenzy, and uttered prophecies'. Every year, a human sacrifice was offered up to the moon-goddess, the victim being struck through the heart with the sacred lance, after which auguries were drawn from his fall and the body trampled underfoot as a means of ritual purification. The moon cult lives on in Georgia to this day, having become merged with that of St George, patron saint of Georgia. St George is often revered as a lunar deity under the name of *Tetri Giorgi* or 'White George', which is also the name adopted by a Georgian nationalist organization active in the 1930's.

We conclude from all this that pagan Iberia and Colchis were centres of an active and varied religious life, in which Anatolian cults of the ancient proto-Georgian tribes merged with elements of popular creeds and with cosmogonies intro-duced from Greece and Zoroastrian Iran to form an original synthesis of ritual and belief, portions of which survived the introduction of Christianity and went underground into the recesses of peasant consciousness, to emerge once more in modern times under the scrutiny of the folklorist and the anthropologist.

CHAPTER V

The Georgian Feudal Monarchy

IT WOULD BE HARD to overestimate the importance of
Georgia's conversion to Christianity, which occurred during
the reign of Constantine the Great, about AD 330, and had the
most far-reaching effect on Georgia's art, literature, culture and
way of life generally. The conversion is ascribed by the Georgian, Greek, Latin and Armenian traditions to a holy slave
woman from Cappadocia named St Nino, who possessed
miraculous powers of healing. She cured the Iberian queen,
Nana, of a mysterious complaint and won her sympathy and
trust. The Georgian king, Mirian by name, was converted in
his turn in the course of a hunting trip during which he found
himself enveloped in pitch darkness (probably through an
eclipse of the sun), and then restored to the light of day when
he invoked the God of the Christians. A church was erected
at the royal city of Mtskheta by divine agency: the central pillar,
which neither machines nor men could lift, was—so the story
goes—miraculously raised into the air and set down upon its
base by invisible power. The original account of the conversion
of the Iberians was written down by the ecclesiastical historian
Rufinus in his Church chronicle composed as early as AD 403,
on the basis of an oral account by a Georgian prince, Bakur,
whom Rufinus had personally met in Palestine. It is thus fairly
authentic as such stories go, which is more than can be said for
other legends embroidered around the saint and her mission by
later Armenian and Georgian scholiasts, who confused Nino's
conversion of Caucasian Iberia with that of Armenia by St
Gregory the Illuminator and the holy Ripsime and her fellow
virgins around AD 301, and incorporated a number of rather
fantastic elements. Even in 1965, so well-informed an author
as the Reverend Michael Bourdeaux, in his *Opium of the*

Fig. 21. Medieval Georgia

A K S

steppe

Terek R.

CHECHNIA

Mt.Kazbek
Daryal
Pass
KHEVSURETI
PSHAVETI
TUSHETI

AVARIA

DAGHESTAN

Derbent

vali

Ananuri

Allaverdi

Telavi

aran

Tbilisi
(Tiflis)

Mtskheta

Sighnaghi

H
E
T
I

Alazani R.

Iori R.

Nukha
(Shekki)

Mtkvari(Kura) R.

Shamakhi

Ganja

A Z E R B A I J A N

Baku

L. Sevan
(Gokcha)

Erivan

hmiadzin

Dvin

K A R A B A G H

Shusha

zid

Nakhchevan

Araxes R.

T A L Y S H

P E R S I A

Tabriz

L. Urmia

S

Urmia

C
a
s
p
i
a
n

S
e
a

—HAS—

People, could refer to Nino as a man, and assert that she was crucified, whereas she died a natural death in the odour of sanctity and was buried at Bodbe in Kakheti province.

Special interest attaches to references in the later accounts to the True Cross and the seamless Coat of Jesus Christ, allegedly retrieved from Mount Golgotha and removed to Mtskheta by the Jews of Georgia, and preserved there after the Crucifixion. This legend has a certain documentary basis in the ancient traditions of the Jewish community in Georgia, amongst whom the Christian faith evidently had adepts even before Nino's mission. Some very ancient Jewish tombstones, discovered in this district of Georgia, have been studied and published by Professor G. V. Tsereteli.

This conversion to Christianity, so full of momentous consequences for the Georgians, was assisted by historical circumstances. A generation previously, Christianity had triumphed in Armenia where, after wreaking hideous atrocities on the person of St Gregory the Illuminator, and murdering Ripsime, Gaiane and their attendant virgins, King Tiridates, after some years of swinish dementia, had finally seen the light. (Gregory's gruesome tortures are depicted to this day on the walls of the Armenian cathedral in New Julfa, close to Isfahan.) We should also recall that by St Nino's time, parts of western Georgia, comprising Colchis, Abkhazia and Lazica, had already been evangelized by missionaries active in the Greek colonies along the Black Sea coast. Although Christianity was not adopted as the state religion of Lazica until the sixth century, the Council of Nicaea in AD 325 was attended by bishops from both Trebi-

Fig. 21

zond, a principal seaport of Lazica, and Bichvinta (Pitiunt), the strategic port and metropolitan see on the Abkhazian coast. By AD 330, political conditions thus strongly favoured the conversion of eastern Georgia also to the new official creed of the Romans, and the Iberian ruling class adopted it without a struggle. The Georgians, with the Armenians, became an outpost of Christendom in the East, their cultural and social life being henceforth deliberately orientated away from the culture of Zoroastrian Iran and later, the Islamic civilization of the Arab world, towards the great centres of Orthodox Christianity, with all that this entailed in the field of social life and material culture generally.

The structure of the Georgian monarchy necessarily underwent fundamental changes as a result of the adoption of Christianity as the state religion. The old pagan kings of Iberia, in Cyril Toumanoff's view, were theophanic monarchs in the Anatolian and Mesopotamian style, and their cosmocratic claims, evolved in the course of the first century of our era, manifested themselves in the title of Great King. They had already advanced far since the days when the *mamasakhlisi* or father of the tribe residing at Mtskheta was revered by his peers as *primus inter pares* among the Georgian dynasts. No doubt the examples of 'Divus Augustus' and Claudius the God, whose friends and allies the Iberian kings were proud to be, encouraged them even further in their pretensions. The cosmological aspect of the Iberian political theophany appears obvious from the number—seven—of the *eristavs* or dukes subordinate to the Iberian Great King at this period, symbolizing so it seems the seven circumsolar planets. The break with the past brought about by Iberia's conversion to Christianity also coincided with the inauguration of a new dynasty in eastern Georgia. The Iberian Arsacids had recently become extinct, and Mirian (later canonized as St Mirian), the first Christian king of Georgia, was also the first ruler of the new Chosroid dynasty, who were themselves a branch of the Iranian Mihranids, one of the seven Great Houses of the Persian Empire.

The Chosroids ruled in Iberia for over two centuries, until the institution of monarchy was abolished for the time being by the Persians in the course of the sixth century. They had a strong sense of family solidarity—the *Life* of Peter the Iberian (a Georgian saintly man prominent in the religious schisms of Byzantium) speaks of Peter's father reigning conjointly with his two uncles 'according to the custom of the Iberian royal house'. However, the royal family had constant difficulty in keeping in check their own unruly vassals. The Crown, naturally enough, regarded the ducal fiefs of Iberia as non-inheritable, exactly as the office of High Constable was non-inheritable; the members of the princely class, who provided the mainstay of the feudal order, tended to treat them as hereditary apanages. The Crown's attempts to control ducal succession were resented and resisted, the consequent tensions contributing to the downfall of the monarchy in the sixth century.

The Georgian feudal system took on definitive shape at this early period, and continued in being right up to the Russian annexation in 1801. It developed features similar to institutions characterizing Western Christendom in the later Middle Ages. In fact, it used to be thought that Georgia's feudal system derived from the influence of the Crusaders, remnants of whom, still clad in medieval chain armour, were mistakenly discerned in the picturesque, old-world Georgian mountain tribe of the Khevsurs. But it is now clear that analogies are rather to be sought in Byzantium and Sasanian Iran, whence the Chosroid dynasty actually hailed. Here, under the Sasanian Great Kings, royal power rested on a delicate balance between feudal allegiance and bureaucratic absolutism. Under the supreme authority of the King of Kings was a motley assemblage of vassal rulers, provincial satraps and *bdeashkh* (or *pitiakhsh* —a title often encountered in old Georgian sources), also chiefs of clans—certain of them hereditary dynasts, others being viceroys appointed by the king. Beneath these were ranged the nobles and knights, some of them vassals of the princes, others owing direct allegiance to the sovereign. At the lower end of the scale came the peasants—free yeomen and serfs, rather than chattel slaves—who followed their lords into battle, and formed

the rank and file of the Persian army. It is of a similar social hierarchy on a smaller scale of which the fifth-century author of the
Martyrdom of Saint Shushanik gives us a glimpse when he speaks
of 'the grandees and noble ladies, the gentry and common folk
of the land of Georgia'.

Whereas the Iberian kings, possibly for reasons of state,
adopted Christianity quite readily, paganism did not give up
its hold on the populace without a struggle. In some cases, it
simply adopted a Christian colouring and went underground,
so to speak, persisting in various guises in remote Caucasian
glens right up to the present day. The *Life of Saint Nino* relates
how King Mirian and one of his dukes 'summoned the mountain clans, men of wild and savage appearance, and preached
the Gospel to them. But they refused to be baptized. So the
royal duke turned the sword on them and cast down their idols
by force. The king laid heavy taxes upon those who did not
wish to receive baptism, who therefore banded together and
became nomads. Some of these were converted by St Abibos
of Nekresi [a holy man of the sixth century], but others have
remained heathen until the present day.' At a place called Kola
in south-western Georgia, a group of heathen parents hurled
their children, aged between seven and nine years, into a pit
and stoned them to death rather than submit to their conversion
to Christianity; these children are numbered among the martyrs
of the Georgian Church.

In some instances, the adoption of Christianity, by imposing
standards of conduct and morality higher than those socially
acceptable to the people of that age, brought with it personal
and domestic problems of an acute kind. An Armenian noble
lady named Shushanik, for example, was married to a Georgian governor, Varsken, who abjured Christianity in favour of
Mazdaism in order to curry favour with the Persians. Shushanik
refused to take part in a carousal where men and women were
eating and drinking together, upon which her depraved husband

'began to utter foul-mouthed insults and kicked her with his foot. Picking up a poker, he crashed it down on her head and split it open and injured one of her eyes. And he struck her face unmercifully with his fist and dragged her to and fro by her hair, bellowing like a wild beast and roaring like a mad-man.' After seven years of such ordeals, eaten up by ulcers and vermin and kept in close captivity, the saintly princess finally expired. Her tormentor Varsken was ultimately put to death by the Georgian King Vakhtang Gorgaslan, who reigned from about 446 to 510, and features in Georgian history as a Caucasian 'King Arthur' of knightly prowess and valiant feats of arms.

At its inception, the Georgian Church was placed under the aegis of the Patriarchs of Antioch, and remained for the next century firmly attached to the Orthodox creed. This allegiance was much strained by the proceedings of the Council of Chalcedon in 451, which formulated the 'official' doctrine on the dual nature of Jesus Christ. Along with the Copts, the Syrians and the Armenians, the Georgians had considerable reservations about accepting the dictates of Chalcedon, which were widely resented in the Eastern Churches. A Georgian prince named Narbarnugios (*c.* 409–488) went to Palestine from Constantinople, became a monk under the name of Peter the Iberian, and built a splendid monastery near Bethlehem, with mosaic pavements embodying the oldest Georgian inscriptions. Peter the Iberian became one of the most formidable opponents of the Orthodox Diophysites, and has even been identified with the mysterious author of the spiritual writings of 'Dionysius the Areopagite'. At the mono-physite Armeno-Georgian Church synod held at Dvin in 506, 24 out of the 33 Georgian bishops were present, and joined with the Armenian and Caucasian Albanians in condemning the dogma of Chalcedon. King Vakhtang Gorgaslan is credited with securing the autocephaly or independent status of the Georgian national Church, which from then onwards (apart from a century's break during the Tsarist period) has elected its own Catholicos-Patriarch, who now resides at Tbilisi and officiates there at the Sioni cathedral and also at the patriarchal cathedral in Mtskheta. During the sixth century, Syrian monophysite refugees, the so-called Syrian Fathers, came to Georgia and founded monastic communities on the Egyptian and Syrian model. Georgian monks early installed themselves at the monastery of St Saba in the Kedron gorge in Palestine, where they celebrated the liturgy in their own tongue.

During the later Sasanian period, in the sixth century, the Iberian monarchy was weakened by civil strife, and also by the struggle between Byzantium and Iran for domination over the Caucasus. After the death of King Vakhtang Gorgaslan in 510, this decline became so marked that the Persian king Khusrau Anushirvan (531–579) was able to abolish the Iberian monarchy and assert direct control over Georgia's internal affairs.

The extinction of royal power in Iberia left a vacuum in the local power structure of the Georgian lands. This gap was filled now by a resurgent monarchy in western Georgia, where royal power had been in abeyance since the days of Mithradates the Great of Pontus, mortal foe of Pompey and the Romans. The new kingdom, whose territory included that of ancient Colchis and much of Pontus itself, was called Lazica, being under the domination of the Laz tribes of the Black Sea coast. In 523, King Tsate of Lazica was baptized, and installed a Byzantine garrison in the mighty fortress of Petra (Tsikhis-dziri), overlooking the Black Sea between Batumi and Kobu-leti. (This magnificent site, rearing up between the Tbilisi-Batumi railway and main road, is at present being excavated by the Batumi Research Institute under its director Mr Aslan Inaishvili, the foundation of the garrison church having already been laid bare.) Throughout the sixth century, Persians and

Byzantines fought for control of Lazica as well as of upland Svaneti, and Petra was the scene of many bloodthirsty engage, ments. The Lazic kings did their best to play off the Persians and Byzantines against one another. They had in fact little reason to prefer the Christian Greeks to the infidel Persians, especially as agents of the emperor Justinian assassinated the able Lazic king Gubaz II in 553. These wars are chronicled in detail by Procopius and his continuator Agathias of Myrina, who provide much valuable information about the historical topography of western Georgia, as well as verbatim reports of speeches and dialogues which provide an unusual insight into the outlook and opinions of the Georgians of those days.

With the monarchy suppressed in Caucasian Iberia, the national cause was strongly espoused by local Georgian princes, who continued to uphold the Christian faith in the provinces of Kartli and Kakheti in spite of pressure from the Persians. The social and political situation in eastern Georgia during the reign of Khusrau Anushirvan is vividly portrayed in the Pas, sion of St Eustace of Mtskheta, composed by an anonymous Georgian hagiographer in the sixth century. Eustace was a Persian cobbler plying his trade in Georgia. Converted to Christianity, he was put to death by the Sasanian *marzpan* or viceroy of Tbilisi in 545, following protests by the Persian shoemakers' trade union in Georgia, who banded together to prevent any of their number from quitting the Zoroastrian religion. Despite such repressions, the Iberian princes Guaram and Stephen I and II took the unusual step of issuing coins modelled on the silver drachms of King Hormizd IV of Iran (579–590), but embodying various independent elements in the design, beginning with the addition of the initials of the respective Georgian princes, and culminating in the substitu, tion of the Christian Cross for the sacred flame normally por, trayed on the Zoroastrian fire,altar on the coin's reverse. This was, of course, a political act of the first magnitude, and points

Plate 74f

to the efforts of Duke Stephen I of Iberia between 590 and 607 to re-establish the political autonomy of eastern Georgia and strengthen the Christian faith. This Duke Stephen I, who received the Byzantine title of Patrikios, is portrayed on one of the sculptures on the eastern façade of the church of Jvari ('the Cross') on a high hill overlooking the Mtkvari valley close to Mtskheta. This classic example of the cruciform domed church, built by Duke Stephen's own architects, is now floodlit at night and provides a splendid vista on the north-western approaches to Tbilisi. It was in Duke Stephen's time also that the Georgian Church finally broke with that of Armenia, and was reunited with that of orthodox Byzantium.

Plates 36, 38

Early in the seventh century, on the eve of the great Arab conquests, the Persians staged one last massive offensive against the Greeks, capturing Jerusalem itself from the Christians in 614. Under the able leadership of Emperor Heraclius, the Byzantines soon recovered from this setback. Heraclius's forces appeared under the walls of Tbilisi, led by the hideous Jibghu, *khaqan* or ruler of the Turkic Khazars who lived along the Volga, and later adopted the Jewish faith. The Persians and Georgians who formed the garrison of Tbilisi, so the Armenian chronicler Movses Daskhuranci relates in his *History of the Caucasian Albanians*, were at first over-confident.

> Although they saw the immense forces of the north and the west surrounding the town like mountains with their four-wheeled balistra and divers other weapons built by Roman engineers with which they unerringly hurled enormous boulders to breach the walls, and although they saw the great bulging hides full of stones and sand with which they caused the river Kura [Mtkvari], which skirts one side of the town, to overflow and dash against the wall, they were not at all dismayed; but encouraging one another, they repaired and rebuilt the damaged parts.

At first, everything went in favour of the besieged, who amused themselves by making a mockery of the Khazar attackers.

They fetched a huge pumpkin upon which they drew the image of the king of the Huns, a cubit broad and a cubit long. In place of his eyelashes which no one could see, they drew a thin line; the region of his beard they left ignomini‚ ously naked, and they made the nostrils a span wide with a number of hairs under them in the form of a moustache so that all might recognize him. This they brought and placed upon the wall opposite them, and showing it to the armies, they called out: 'Behold the Emperor, your King! Turn and worship him, for it is Jibghu Khaqan!' And seizing a spear, they stuck it into the pumpkin which caricatured him before them, and they mocked and jeered and reviled the other king [*i.e.* Heraclius], and called him a foul sodomite.

Temporarily worsted, the Greeks and Khazars retired to gather reinforcements. In the next year, 627, they returned and succeeded in taking the town and citadel of Tbilisi. Khaqan Jibghu celebrated the event by flaying alive the Persian and Georgian commanders of Tbilisi fortress, and sending their skins, stuffed with straw, to Emperor Heraclius as a trophy of this warlike excursion.

The triumph of Heraclius and his Greeks and Khazars proved irrelevant to the long‚term historical evolution of Chris‚ tian Caucasia. Under the Prophet Muhammad, the Arabs were already on the move to world dominance. Weakened by two centuries of religious schism, Byzantium was in no state to resist their inexorable advance. The caliphate of Omar (634– 644) saw Islam's transformation from a religious sect to an imperial power. The chief events of his reign were the defeat of the Persians at Kadisiya in 637 and the conquest of Syria and Palestine. The taking of Egypt followed, and the final rout of the Persians at Nehawend in 641 brought Iran under Arab rule. Omar was assassinated by a Persian slave in 644, but by this time the Arabs had already made their appearance in Armenia (640) and Kartli (642–643). Erzerum, the great Byzantine stronghold in eastern Anatolia, was seized by the Arabs in 654, and the whole of Armenia was in their hands. The Georgians saw no advantage in holding out, and proffered their voluntary submission. An Arab *amir* or viceroy was in-stalled in Tbilisi, to rule Kartli and the rest of eastern Georgia in the caliph's name.

Arab rule proved as unpopular in Georgia as had been that of Byzantium and Sasanian Iran. The eighth-century writer Ioane Sabanisdze complained that 'we faithful Christians are enslaved, enduring persecution and privation, chained by poverty as if by iron fetters, suffering and pining away beneath the onerous tribute which they exact.' The Tbilisi townspeople organized masquerades and carnivals in which they made fun of the habits of their Muslim overlords—anticipating the pro-cession known as *Qeenoba* which became such a feature of Plate 3 Tbilisi life in the eighteenth and nineteenth centuries. To keep the rebellious Georgians under control, the caliphs of Baghdad despatched a number of punitive expeditions, the most notori-ous being that of 736–738 headed by Merwan or Murvan Qru ('the Deaf'), as he is called in Georgian sources, alluding to this commander's refusal to listen to any plea for mercy by the vanquished. It was this Murvan who destroyed the ancient cita-del of the Iberian kings at Mtskheta-Armazi, dating from Graeco-Roman times.

Patriotic and religious issues apart, the Arab domination in Georgia produced a remarkable resurgence in the fortunes of the new capital city of eastern Georgia, Tbilisi—Tiflis in the Arabic and European sources. The name of the city derives from Georgian *tbili* 'warm', an allusion to the natural hot springs for which the city was famed. (Compare Teplice in

Bohemia, Baden Baden in Germany, or Aquae Sulis—Bath Spa—in south-west England.) According to tradition, it was King Vakhtang Gorgaslan who removed the capital of Kartli in 458 some twenty miles from Mtskheta to the south-east down the Mtkvari valley to the present-day Tbilisi, which had been an inhabited settlement throughout the Bronze and Iron Ages in Caucasia. It soon became a great international emporium, at the junction of several busy trade routes. In the bazaars were bought and sold silk from Shirvan, furs from Russia, inlaid metal work and carpets from Daghestan, and countless other commodities. Tbilisi became an important centre for both

Plate 73

Muslim and Jewish learning, and several medieval treatises of considerable interest were written there. Not for nothing could the Armenian chronicler Movses Daskhuranci refer with admiration to 'the luxurious, prosperous, famous and great commercial city of Tiflis'.

In the year 912, mention is made of a lieutenant of the caliph in Tbilisi by the name of Jafar ibn 'Ali. Following the disin-tegration of the 'Abbasid caliphate towards the middle of the tenth century, control over the city and district of Tbilisi re-mained vested for two centuries in this Jafar's line. These Jafarids struck coins in their own name, and one of them pil-laged the treasury of the cathedral of the Life-Giving Pillar at Mtskheta. By 1122, the affairs of the Jafarid family had 'become ruined and got into confusion', as a result of which this Muslim enclave fell an easy prey to the Georgian king David the Builder (1089–1125), who captured it after a brief siege. After three days' pillage, David granted an amnesty to the Muslim in-habitants; 'he soothed their hearts', as the contemporary Arabic chronicler Ibn al-Azraq writes, and 'left them alone, in all goodness'. David even spared their religious susceptibilities by forbidding the pork-loving Georgians to bring pigs into the Muslim quarter of the town. His successor Dimitri I (1125–54) struck coins with his own monogram on one side, and the

Fig. 22. Royal arms of the Bagratid dynasty. An eighteenth-century treatment, showing the seamless coat of Jesus Christ (centre), David's harp and sling, royal orb and crossed swords, St George and the Dragon, and the scales of justice

name of the Muslim caliph and the Seljuk sultan on the reverse. Dimitri was a tolerant monarch; though a strictly orthodox Christian, he would attend the Friday service at the Tbilisi mosque, being seated on a platform opposite the preacher, and used to present the mullah with two hundred gold pieces on his departure. This religious and racial tolerance is characteristic of the easy-going Georgian character, in spite of the terrible perse-cutions endured from Muslim and pagan neighbours over the centuries.

While the Saracens held sway in Tbilisi and the Georgian monarchy was in eclipse, a vigorous ruling family was rising to eminence in the marchlands of Georgia and Armenia. This was the clan of the Bagratids, who were to unify Georgia under a single sceptre and reign there for a full thousand years. The Bagratids claimed for prestige purposes to be descended from David and Solomon of Israel. This legend was already current by the time of Prince Ashot the Great (780–826), who mi-grated from Armenia and settled at Artanuji in Tao (south-western Georgia), receiving from the Byzantine emperor the title of Kuropalates or 'Guardian of the Palace'. Thus we find Ashot's father-confessor St Gregory of Khandzta (759–861) addressing Ashot as: 'Monarch, you who are called the son of the divinely anointed prophet David', while the Byzantine

Fig. 22

emperor Constantine Porphyrogenitus (912–959) also refers with approbation in his treatise *De Administrando Imperio* to this Bagratid claim, as being a reliable historical tradition. A modern student of the question, Sir Steven Runciman, also supports its authenticity, partly, it seems, because of the fact that an eccentric Georgian princess at the court of Tsar Nicholas II of Russia (1894–1917) was in the habit of wearing mourning at the feast of the Assumption of the Virgin Mary which was, so she said, a family affair! More serious research indicates that the Bagratids were in fact of ancient and respectable Caucasian lineage, being originally princes of Speri (Ispir) in the upper Chorokhi valley north of Erzerum, and having a castle at the modern Bayburt. Sumbat I Bagratuni was Master of the Horse and coronant of Armenia as early as 288–301, and the families retained the highest dignities of state in the Armenian kingdom for many centuries thereafter. In the eighth century, the Bagrations spread northwards into Georgia and revitalized its political life and social structure. They reigned in their new home right up to the accession of the Russian tsar Alexander I in 1801—in Imereti, they retained power until 1810—surely a world record for continuous rule by any one dynastic family.

From the beginning of Bagratid rule in Georgia stems a special system of national chronology, which has been extensively studied by the late E. S. Taqaishvili. The Armenians had earlier marked their break with Byzantium and the Greek Orthodox Church by introducing a national era which begins in AD 552 and runs continuously thereafter. The Georgians, for reasons which have nothing to do with religious schism, introduced their own new system from the end of AD 780, reckoning on the basis of the so-called *Koronikon* or Paschal cycle of 532 years. This cycle is obtained by multiplying nineteen lunar years by twenty-eight solar years, producing the *Paschalion* or Perpetual Calendar, on the basis of which Easter Day and the other movable holy days of the Christian Church are fixed. It is a perpetual calendar, because when one cycle of 532 years ends, regardless from which year reckoning is begun, all the holy days in the next cycle fall in the same months, in the same weeks, and on the same days of the week as in the previous cycle. In treatises on the ancient calendar by Georgian writers, this cycle is called *Asuruli*, *i.e.* Syrian, because it is taken over from the Syrian Church.

Having adopted the calculation of time according to the *Koronikon*, Georgians adopted at the same time a special chrono﹍logy from the Creation of the World to the Birth of Christ. According to Georgian reckoning, 5,604 years elapsed from the Creation to Christ's birth, that is, 96 more years than the Greeks reckoned (setting the Creation in 5,508 BC), or 104 and 112 more years than the Alexandrian and Pandoran reckon﹍ings respectively. According to the official calendar of the Georgian Orthodox Church, 7,570 years have now (in AD 1966) elapsed since the beginning of the World. The current 15th *Koronikon* began at the end of 1844, so that we are now in the 122nd year of the Georgian Paschal Cycle.

In their struggle against the Arab caliphs, the Byzantine emperors courted the allegiance of the Bagratids and other dynasts of Armenia and Georgia, conferring on them grandiose titles and abundant largesse, including richly enamelled icons of which several survive in the Georgian State Museum of Art. In 888, Adarnase IV Bagration revived the Iberian monarchy, dormant for over three centuries, and assumed the title of King of the Georgians. The influence of the Georgians in Byzantium became strong in the tenth century, when John﹍Varazvache Chordvaneli and his son Euthymius founded the Iviron or Georgian Monastery on Mount Athos. This foundation is linked with a number of interesting historical events, notably the formidable revolt of Bardas Scleros in 976, directed against the young emperors Basil II and his brother Constantine VIII. One of the Georgian monks on Mount Athos was a certain

Plate 62

John Tornik, a retired general of exceptional vigour and prowess. The Greek court was in despair at the rebels' success, until they bethought themselves of recalling John Tornik from his monastic retreat. Tornik rode straight to Georgia, to prince David Kuropalates of Tao, who gave him twelve thousand picked horsemen, with whose aid Tornik put Bardas Scleros to flight. In return for this signal service, Basil II granted certain eastern provinces of his empire in Byzantine Armenia to David Kuropalates to hold during his lifetime; on Tornik and his brethren the Byzantine court conferred sundry privileges and immunities, along with rich endowments. The Life of Saint Euthymius the Athonite, written by his successor Saint George the Hagiorite (1009–65), contains fascinating details of these events, and does much to dispel the biased account in the Byzantine Greek sources, according to which Scleros was defeated by another Greek general, Bardas Phocas. It is sad to read that after all this excitement, General Tornik found it impossible to settle down again to quiet monastic life, and had to be reproved by Prior John for gossiping with admiring visitors and 'chatting and listening to tales about warlike adventures'. Relapsing into gloomy silence, the monastery's chief benefactor 'ended his days in a life of sanctity and eventually departed towards his Lord and Maker'.

Being childless, the great David Kuropalates of Tao adopted as heir presumptive a scion of the Bagration family, named Bagrat. Through his mother this prince (the future King Bagrat III) was also the eventual claimant to the throne of Abasgia (Abkhazia), as the old west Georgian state, formerly Lazica or Colchis, was now officially styled. With the support of David Kuropalates and the Duke of Kartli Ioane Marushisdze, Bagrat III went from strength to strength. He won the throne of Kartli in 975 and then, in 978, acquired that of Abasgia as well. In 989, Bagrat overcame the powerful dynast of Trialeti—the district famed centuries earlier for its magnificent Bronze

Age culture—who rejoiced in the name of Rati Bagvashi, thus inspiring other unruly feudal vassals with proper respect for royal authority.

On the death of David Kuropalates in 1001, Bagrat further succeeded him as ruler of Tao; seven years later, Bagrat's own father, Gurgen II, died, leaving him the provinces of Shav-sheti, Klarjeti, Samtskhe and Javakheti. Only the city of Tbilisi itself, with its Muslim *amirs*, and the small eastern king-dom of Kakheti-Hereti remained outside his grasp. This trend towards political unity was powerfully aided by the dynamic leadership of the Georgian Orthodox Church, who realized that feudal turbulence and division could only serve to streng-then Georgia's pagan and infidel neighbours. In 951, the bio-grapher of St Gregory of Khandzta, Giorgi Merchule, de-clared proudly: 'Georgia is reckoned to consist of those spacious lands in which church services are celebrated and all prayers said in the Georgian tongue.' Far away, on Mount Sinai, the Georgian scribe John Zosime composed in Saint Catharine's Monastery a eulogy in praise of the Georgian language, which provides eloquent witness to the patriotic consciousness of lead-ing intellectuals of that age.

The sudden aggrandizement of the Bagratid dynasty soon provoked violent reaction in Byzantium. The Greeks were indignant at the Georgians' refusal to hand back the territories temporarily ceded to David Kuropalates as a reward for crush-ing Bardas Scleros, which should strictly speaking have re-verted to Emperor Basil II when David died in 1001. For some years Basil bided his time. He was engaged in an exhausting and bloodthirsty war against the Bulgarians, who menaced the very existence of the Byzantine state. In 1014, the year in which Bagrat III of Georgia died, Basil overwhelmingly defeated the Bulgarians, which he celebrated by blinding the 15,000 pri-soners and leaving a single one-eyed man to every hundred to lead them back to their tsar, who fainted and expired at the

Fig. 23. (a) Bowman; (b) quiver. Detail from Georgian medieval manuscripts. After L. A. Shervashidze

a

b

Plate 74g

sight. Basil the Bulgar-Slayer ('Bulgaroktonos') then turned his attention to the East. In 1021 he invaded Georgia and defeated the young king Giorgi I, annexing Tao, Kola, Arda- han and even Javakheti. Giorgi died in 1027, and the war con- tinued under his son Bagrat IV (1027–72). Eventually Bagrat made his peace with the Emperor Romanus III Argyrus (1028– 1034), who gave his own daughter Helen in marriage to the Georgian king in token of peace and friendship.

Fresh trouble between Georgia and Byzantium broke out under the Emperor Constantine Monomachus (1042–54), who, with incredible folly and shortsightedness, abolished and annexed the Christian kingdom of Armenia, and would have done the same to Georgia but for the desperate resistance of the king and people. None the less, Bagrat IV continued to bear the Byzantine titles of Nobilissimos and Sebastos, and struck silver coins portraying the image of the Blachernae Virgin. This design, taken from that of the celebrated Constantinople icon, was earlier extensively used on the coins of Constantine Monomachus himself.

Four centuries earlier, under Emperor Heraclius, the inter- necine struggle between the Byzantines and the Sasanian Per- sians in the Caucasus had resulted in an easy conquest of Georgia and Armenia by the Arabs. A precisely comparable series of disasters now followed this Greek aggression in Ar- menia and the Near East. During the 1060's, the Seljuk Turks from Central Asia, having captured most of Persia with con- siderable ease, surged westwards with the intent of occupying Anatolia and the heartlands of Byzantium itself. They cap- tured the Armenian capital of Ani in 1064, the demoralized Armenians, disorganized by Byzantine oppression, offering only token resistance. In 1066, the Seljuks raided Javakheti and devastated the important Georgian centre of Akhalkalaki ('New Town'); two years later they laid waste the provinces of Kartli and Argveti. The final débacle of eastern Christendom occurred in 1071, when the forces of Seljuk Sultan Alp-Arslan dealt a crushing defeat to the Byzantines at Manazkert immedi- ately to the north of Lake Van, capturing the Emperor Romanus IV Diogenes, who died in misery soon after his release. King Bagrat IV of Georgia died in the following year (1072), when suzerainty over the troubled and ravaged land of Georgia passed to his son Giorgi II.

The new king proved incompetent, and his reign witnessed a series of ignominious capitulations to the Turks and to various unruly feudal lords who rebelled against their king. In 1089 Giorgi II abdicated in favour of his sixteen-year-old son David. The young David IV, known as *Aghmashenebeli* or 'The Builder', soon proved himself a ruler and military leader of outstanding ability. He organized troops of picked cavalry, which he trained in person, arrested and exiled the ringleader of the rebellious barons, Duke Liparit Bagvashi, and in 1096 discontinued payment of tribute to the Turkish Sultan. He was assisted in his policies by the timely arrival of the Crusaders in Asia Minor and Syria in 1097, and by their capture of Jeru- salem and the Holy Land from the Saracens in 1099. Between 1110 and 1122, David won a series of brilliant victories over the Seljuks, culminating in the great battle of Didgori in 1121 and the fall of Tbilisi to the Georgians the following year. The Georgian army at this time was reinforced by 40,000 fierce Qipchaks from the north Caucasian steppes, and also, accord- ing to one account, by several hundred Frankish volunteers from the ranks of the Crusaders. With their aid, David extended the frontiers of Georgia far beyond her historical

a

Fig. 24. Maces, (a) from MS. H 1665 of Institute of Manuscripts, Tbilisi, fifteenth century; (b) from a manuscript in the Kutaisi Historical-Ethnographic Museum

b

boundaries, taking in much of Armenia with the city of Ani, Shirvan with the city of Shamakhi, the foothills of Daghestan as far as Derbent, also Ossetia and Abkhazia.

A patron of the arts and sciences, David the Builder found time for many educational and cultural innovations. Close to Kutaisi in Imereti, the ancient city of Medea and King Aeëtes, David founded the monastery, cathedral and academy of Gelati, under the direction of the illustrious Georgian neo-Platonist Ioane Petritsi. He carried through a far-reaching re-organization of the Georgian Church, culminating in the Synod of Ruisi-Urbnisi in 1103, which adopted stricter canons of ecclesiastical law and ordained the deposition of a number of venal and corrupt clerics. Under David's leadership, trade flourished and national unity was restored; his premature death in January 1125 was mourned throughout the nation.

Fig. 25. Sword in scabbard, from MS. H 1665 of Institute of Manuscripts, Tbilisi. Fifteenth century.

Figs. 23–25

King David the Builder and his successors made Georgia a power to be reckoned with in international affairs. Around 1225, Patriarch Jacques de Vitry of Jerusalem wrote: 'There is also in the East another Christian people, who are very warlike and valiant in battle, being strong in body and powerful in the countless numbers of their warriors. They are much dreaded by the Saracens and have often by their invasions done great damage to the Persians, Medes and Assyrians on whose borders they dwell, being entirely surrounded by infidel nations. These men are called Georgians, because they especially revere and worship St George, whom they make their patron and standard-bearer in their fight with the infidels, and they honour him above all other saints. Whenever they come on pilgrimage to the Lord's Sepulchre, they march into the Holy City with banners displayed, without paying tribute to anyone, for the Saracens dare in no wise molest them. They wear their hair and beards about a cubit long and have hats upon their heads.' (It is not true that the name 'Georgians' derives from St George; as already explained, it is connected with the Arabic and

Fig. 26

Fig. 26. Georgian late medieval hat styles, fifteenth to seventeenth centuries. After L. A. Shervashidze.

Persian ethnic name *Kurj* or *Gurj*.) The Georgians were commonly known in Palestine as 'Christians of the Girdle', supposedly because their patron saint used his girdle to bind up the dragon's body after he had killed it with his lance. On the Saracen side, the Arab authority al-'Umari (d. 1348) describes the Georgians as 'the kernel of the religion of the Cross', adding that the Mameluke Sultans of Egypt were in the habit of addressing rescripts to the Georgian king to 'the great monarch, the hero, the bold, just to his subjects, the successor of the Greek kings, protector of the homeland of the knights, supporter of the faith of Jesus, the anointed leader of Christian heroes, the best of close companions, and the friend of kings and sultans'. For their part, the Georgian sovereigns emphasized their role as Defenders of the Faith by defiantly inscribing their coins in Arabic and Persian with the titles 'Sword of the Messiah' or 'Champion of the Messiah'. Another Patriarch of Jerusalem, the Orthodox Dorotheus I, wrote that 'the pious kings of Iberia have always been the protectors of the Holy Sepulchre', where in fact they ranked fourth of the national Churches, owning not only the Chapel of the Invention of the Cross, but even, for a time, that of Calvary itself. They lost their separate representation in the seventeenth century because they could no longer afford the tribute exacted by the Turkish government from all tenants of the Sepulchre, and many of their splendid medieval vestments now adorn the Treasury of the Orthodox.

Plate 74 1, 1, m

113

Fig. 27

Fig. 28

The great work of David the Builder was ably continued by his great-granddaughter Queen Tamar (1184–1213), who was appointed co-regnant of Georgia already in 1178 by her father Giorgi III, during his own lifetime. Tamar married first of all a dissolute scion of the Russian Bogolyubskoi family of Suzdal, whom she eventually divorced for sexual misconduct of an unnatural kind and expelled from the kingdom, though not without bloody civil strife. In 1189 Tamar married David Soslan, an Ossetian prince with Bagration blood in his veins. She bore him the future King Giorgi Lasha (1213–23) and Queen Rusudan (1223–45). At the outset of Tamar's reign, there was a movement to limit the royal prerogative by setting up a kind of House of Lords, with authority matching that of the sovereign. Unlike the efforts of the barons under King John, Tamar's English contemporary, this Georgian constitutional movement came to naught; it seems to have been devoid of popular support, and had as its aim the substitution for the relatively popular monarchy of a system of oligarchy which would certainly have been even more oppressive for the urban proletariat and peasant classes.

Among the many political and military triumphs of Tamar's glorious reign, special interest attaches to the foundation of the Empire of Trebizond. This came about as a result of the capture and sacking of Constantinople in 1204 by an army of Frankish desperadoes and freebooters styling themselves the Fourth Crusade. The Byzantine empire being thus dismembered, Tamar and her Georgians occupied Trebizond and areas of the Black Sea coast still further westward. A scion of

Fig. 27. Monogram of Queen Tamar (1184–1213), formed from the letters TAMAR in the Georgian knightly hand (mkhedruli). As employed on copper coinage of the reign

Fig. 28. Court robes of King Giorgi III (1156–84) and Queen Tamar (1184–1213). From contemporary frescoes at the Vardzia monastery

the imperial family of the Komneni, Alexius, who had been educated in Georgia, was placed at the head of the new and independent empire of Trebizond, which continued its exis‑tence right up to the year 1461, when the city was taken by the Ottoman Sultan Muhammad II. It is interesting to note that local imitations of the silver aspers of Trebizond, known as *Kirmaneuli* after Kyr or Emperor Manuel who reigned from 1238 to 1263, formed the basic coinage of western Georgia for about two centuries. In 1208, the Georgians sent an expedi‑tionary force into Persia and occupied Ardebil; they later raided Tabriz and Kazvin. A Georgian dynasty, the Besh‑kenids, ruled the important town and district of Ahar in Persian Azerbaijan for several generations.

At its apogee the Georgian kingdom was a political organ‑ism of great complexity, with a large bureaucracy and sophisti‑cated social hierarchy. The monarch ruled by the doctrine of divine right, though strong feudal institutions prevented the royal power from degenerating into sheer despotism. The central administration was headed by five senior *vazirs* or ministers: the High Chancellor (an office long associated with the dignity of Archbishop of Tchqondidi), the War Minister, the Lord Chamberlain, the Chancellor of the Exchequer, and the Ata-bag or High Constable, each with a staff of subordinate officials. This administrative structure has been especially well analyzed by W. E. D. Allen in his *History of the Georgian People*, on the basis of contemporary charters and other documents. The *eristavis* or dukes who ruled the provinces were nominally subject to removal by the sovereign; when they died, their heir was supposed to submit their sword of office to the king, and await the sovereign's pleasure. In practice, it usually proved hard for any Georgian monarch to remove such vassals from their rocky castles without resorting to civil war. It is interesting to note that several official titles, through long tenure in one princely line, actually became used as regular surnames, for instance Amilakhvari, originally 'Master of the Royal Stables', Amirejibi, 'Master of the Chamber', Meghvinet-ukhutsesi, 'Chief Wine Steward', as well as Eristavi or 'Duke', with its common Russianized form Eristov.

The Orthodox Church of Georgia bulked large in the country's life, and battling bishops led their troops into the fray alongside the armies of the king. The Church had wide powers of jurisdiction in the field of morals and private conduct, a monopoly of education, as well as enormous economic privileges, grants of land, and valuable immunities and benefactions.

In Tamar's time, the Georgian feudal system reached its high point; fiefs, and arrière fiefs, allodium and immunity, vassalage, investiture and homage—all these familiar terms of Western feudalism had their equivalents in the social system of medieval Georgia. The nation was divided into the categories of *patroni* (from Latin *patronus*) and *qma*, which could mean alternatively vassal or serf—hence the Georgian word for feudalism, *patron-*

qmoba. One of the features of the new centralized power of the
Georgian state at this period was a marked deterioration in
status of the free husbandmen or *mdabiuri*—a class whose importance had already been stressed by Strabo in Classical times.
By the reign of Tamar, the increasing power of the *aznauris* or
squires, the bishops and priors, and the royal officials and tax-
collectors was imposing intolerable strains on these yeomen
farmers, who also bore the brunt of many expensive wars.
The majority were eventually reduced to a semi-servile condition, though the highlanders of the Caucasus mountains
retained their traditional liberties right up to the end of the
monarchy in 1801.

Among the dues and services which might be required of the
Georgian serf were working a stipulated number of days on the
lord's private land, helping to build the lord's house or barns,
handing over a share of the harvest or of his flocks and herds,
offering hospitality to the lord's guests and their retinue, gathering and delivering firewood, and providing food and wine for
the lord's table on the occasion of weddings and Church
festivals. In return, the serf was normally guaranteed possession
of his home and plot of land, protected against marauders by
the lord's private army, and often furnished with a charter or
sigeli, specifying the precise nature of his rights and duties. Such
protected status was indeed often vitally necessary for physical
survival in those turbulent times.

This hierarchical division of Georgian feudal society was
later codified by King Vakhtang VI (1711–24) in an official
table of *wergild* or blood money rates, which had the force of
law. The lives of the highest social class after the king, that of
senior princes and dukes, were valued at 1,536 tumans apiece
(15,360 silver roubles), while peasants or small tradesmen were
valued at only twelve tumans—less than a hundredth part. This
scale of indemnity payments applied only to cases where an
individual was slain by another of equivalent social grade. If a

peasant or squire were audacious enough to slay a prince or a bishop, he would have to pay a higher tariff, and probably be put to death or mutilated as well. Obviously, there were many instances where powerful barons killed defenceless peasants, and avoided paying any blood money at all.

A remarkable feature of Georgian judicial procedure was the system of ordeals, which no doubt derived from ancient Iran, though they have features in common with the ordeals familiar in Western Christendom. In Georgia, the presumed guilt or innocence of an accused party could be established by single combat; by the ordeals of boiling water and red-hot iron; by solemn oath upon an icon; or by a peculiar ritual known as saddling oneself with sin, in which the accused would take the plaintiff on his back and declare: 'May God hold me responsible for thy sins at the Last Judgement, and may I be judged in thy place, if this deed has really been committed by me!' These ordeals continued in use right up to the eighteenth century.

CHAPTER VI

Early Medieval Architecture
and the Arts

THE GEORGIANS, who inhabit one of the most beautiful countries in the world, are blessed with a strong
aesthetic sense. Their art and architecture throughout the ages
combine the practical and the picturesque to a remarkable
degree. Domestic pottery and textiles are almost invariably noteworthy for their decorative qualities. Georgian jewellers and
potters today are still turning out exquisite reproductions and
original creations, inspired by artistic forms dating back in
some cases to the culture of the Bronze Age Georgian tribes.
The twentieth-century visitor, however intent on studying the
effects of modern technology on Georgian industry, agriculture
and education, can scarcely stir a mile without being brought
face to face with a fine church, a ruined castle, an ancient
bridge, even an entire city carved out of the solid rock.

Georgian architecture, ancient and modern, shows remarkable adaptability. Classical travellers, we have noted, spoke of
the Mossynoeci tribe living by the Black Sea in wooden towers
(*mossynes*), whence their name. Such structures are appropriate
to conditions of life in marshy, low-lying coastal districts. In
Guria, wooden houses constructed on similar lines are common today, the dwelling area being supported on solid wooden
stilts. The family climb a step-ladder on to a platform, giving
access to the human living quarters, while the pigs, hens and
other livestock scuffle on the damp earth beneath.

Another form of Georgian popular architecture with a long
history is the rustic house known as *darbazi*, the central feature *Fig. 30*
of which is a pyramidal corbelled cupola (*gvirgvini*) made of
hewn logs and beams, the bottom layer being laid horizontally

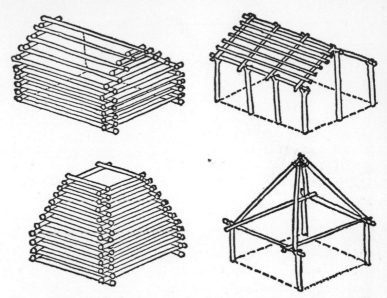

Fig. 29. Basic principles for the construction of Georgian wooden peasant houses. After L. Sumbadze

Fig. 29

with ends overlapping to form a rectangle or octagon upon which successive layers of logs are then piled up to form a tapering structure culminating in an aperture at the summit, to serve as both chimney and window. No less an authority than Vitruvius includes in his *Ten Books on Architecture* a description of the ancient prototype of this Georgian *darbazi*:

> Among the Colchians in Pontus, where there are forests in plenty, they lay down entire trees flat on the ground to the right and the left, leaving between them a space to suit the length of the trees, and they then place above them another pair of trees, resting on the ends of the former and at right angles with them. These four trees enclose the space for the dwelling.—Then upon these they place sticks of timber, one after the other on the four sides, crossing each other at the angles, and so, proceeding with their walls of trees laid

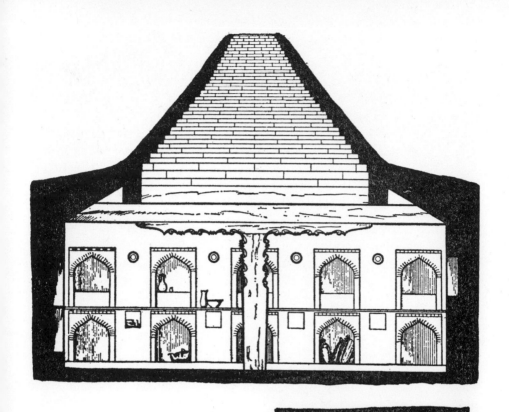

Fig. 30. Plan and section of a traditional Georgian
darbazi *house*

perpendicularly above the lowest, they build up high towers. The interstices, which are left on account of the thickness of the building material, are stopped up with chips and mud. As for the roofs, by cutting away the ends of the cross beams and making them converge gradually as they lay them across, they bring them up to the top from the four sides in the shape of a pyramid. They cover it with leaves and mud and thus construct the roofs of their towers in a rude form of the 'tortoise' style. (Vitruvius, trans. M. H. Morgan, p. 39).

Figs. 30, 31   This mode of construction, sometimes known as 'lantern' vaulting, is also found in Afghanistan. Today, the *darbazi* house, with local variations, occurs extensively in the Georgian provinces of Kartli, Meskheti and Javakheti. These *dar-*
Figs. 32, 33   *bazis* frequently have beautifully carved wooden doors, lintels,

Fig. 31 Georgian darbazi *house, detail*

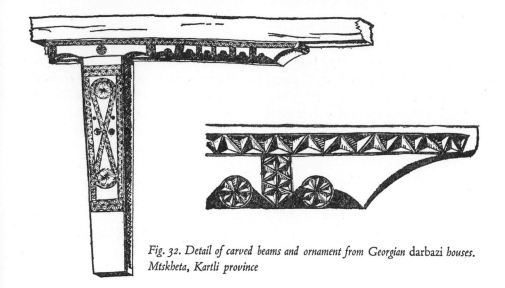

Fig. 32. Detail of carved beams and ornament from Georgian darbazi houses. Mtskheta, Kartli province

fireplaces, also fine hand-carved seats and chests, the techniques showing points of affinity with the stone carving which is such a feature of Georgian churches. Particular care is lavished on the solid wooden upright known as the *deda-bodzi* ('mother-pillar'), which takes the weight of the corbelled roofing.

In Svaneti, situated in the mountains, the traditional peasant house incorporates a high stone tower, with embrasures from which enemy tribesmen could be espied from afar off, and wel-comed suitably with bow and arrow, flint-lock gun or rifle as the case might be.

Plate 1

Georgia is rich in remains of public buildings and palaces, ranging from the vast Graeco-Roman edifices of Mtskheta-Armazi, complete with baths, forums and theatre, and the ancient walled town of Ujarma in Kakheti, to the grandiose medieval palace of Geguti, winter headquarters of the Georgian kings during the eleventh and twelfth centuries, which now stands desolate on a vast plain south of Kutaisi. From the later medieval period, we have the well-preserved feudal castle of

Fig. 34
Plate 57

Ananuri, on the Caucasian military road north of Tbilisi, and Gremi, palace-citadel of the kings of Kakheti, perched on a mighty rock close to the foothills of Daghestan. Above the ancient caravan route leading through Kakheti to Tbilisi and westwards through Gori towards the Black Sea, countless ruined donjons and castle keeps bear witness to the warlike activities of medieval barons, who held merchants to ransom and foreign foes at bay with fine impartiality. A good example of this type of architecture is Manavi, in Outer Kakheti, as well as the fourteenth-century castles at Khertvisi and Adsquri in Samtskhe. One ruined fort on the Gori road bears the picturesque name of 'Kiss my Backside!', this being the retort shouted by a defiant Georgian garrison to a Turkish army which bade them surrender.

Plate 2

Georgia's rocky and mountainous configuration is peculiarly suited to underground or cliff dwellings. Many of these are of natural origin, and provided ideal quarters for Stone Age

Fig. 33. An example of Abkhazian artistic wood-carving. Modern period

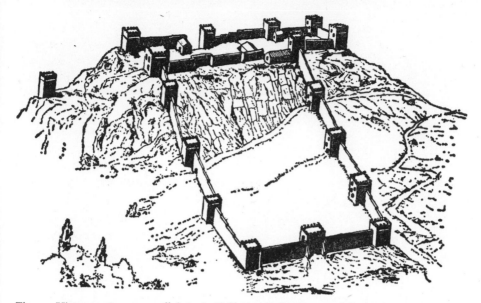

Fig. 34. Ujarma, an important walled city in Kakheti, with fortifications of the fourth century AD. *Reconstruction by Irakli Tsitsishvili*

man. Others, such as the city of Uplistsikhe, were quarried out stage by stage during the Bronze Age and the Graeco-Roman period. This type of construction reached its apogee during the twelfth century with the completion of the breath-taking rock city of Vardzia, in the upper Mtkvari valley close to the modern Turkish frontier. Vardzia numbers at least five hundred rooms and apartments, including chapels, banqueting halls, wine cellars, stables, all connected with a labyrinth of stairs and passages. It is made up of a number of storeys, being cut out of a high vertical cliff face. The royal chapel is decorated with frescoes, traces of which remain to this day. Many refined touches testify to the ingenuity of the Georgian medieval mind. The visitor is still shown a small recess directly above the low and narrow passage leading into the royal dining room; there is a hole just large enough for a lance to be driven down into

Plates 31, 32

Plate 55
Fig. 35

Plate 56

Fig. 35. Thirteenth-century wine-press from the cave monastery at Vardzia. After Givi Gaprindashvili

a man's neck as he passed stooping on his way in to dinner, thus sparing the king the presence of any unwelcome guest.

Vardzia was devastated by the Safavi Shah Tahmasp in 1552. The contemporary Persian historian Hasan-i-Rumlu describes this event in his 'Fairest of Chronicles' (*Ahsan al-Tawarikh*):

> In strength, it was like the wall of Alexander and the castle of Khaybar. In the middle of the fort they had hollowed out a place ten cubits high, and made a church of four rooms and a long bench, and had painted its walls without and within with gold and lapis lazuli and pictures of idols [*i.e.*

frescoes of Christian saints], and arranged a throne in the second room, and an idol [*i.e.* icon] gilt and covered with precious stones, with two rubies for the eyes of that lifeless form; within the church was a narrow way one hundred and fifty cubits long to go up, cut in the solid rock. They had two hidden kiosks for use in time of trouble, and there were doors of iron and steel in the outer rooms, and a golden door in the inner ones. Then the Ghazis [warriors of Islam] fell upon that place and climbed above that fort, and slew the men, and took captive their wives and children. The Shah and his nobles went to see the church, and they slew twenty evil priests, and broke the bell of seventeen maunds weight [about 1500 lb] seven times cast, and destroyed the doors of iron and gold, and sent them to the treasury. . . . Thus the Shah got great booty; and in it were two rubies being the eyes of the idol, each worth fifty tumans [several hundred pounds sterling]. And they levelled the fort to the ground.

Fig. 36. Triple basilica at Zegani, Kakheti. Ground-plan. Over-all length 28.5 m. After G. N. Chubinashvili

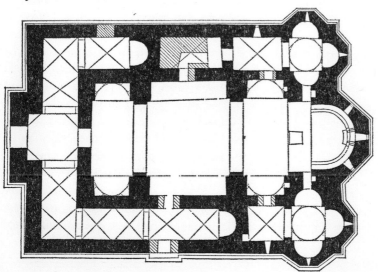

During this same expedition, the near-by underground fortress of Tmogvi was also thoroughly plundered and demolished. Vardzia is now being restored by the Georgian Academy of Sciences. In view of these repeated excesses by Georgia's powerful foes, it is miraculous that so many art treasures and monuments of ancient architecture still survive, even in mutilated form, to this day.

Exciting as the monuments of Georgian secular architecture are, it was in church building that the Georgians, with the Armenians, have been most successful in developing independent and original forms of design and construction technique. The earliest churches, like that of St Nino at Mtskheta, were of wood and perished long ago. In the sixth century, St David of Garesja and his disciple Dodo began work on the subterranean monastery of David Garesja in Outer Kakheti. The earliest conventional stone-built churches, dating mostly from the fifth to the eighth century, belong to the vaulted basilica type, and are the result of contacts with the Christians of Mesopotamia and Syria. The Transcaucasian basilicas may have a single nave, but often there are three; in one unusual variant, these are completely cut off from one another by continuous walls. The most common type, however, has a double row of pillars dividing the space longitudinally into nave and aisles, each separately vaulted. In correspondence with this internal division, the slope of the roof is broken by a short vertical stretch located above the two rows of pillars. The important cathedrals of Bolnisi and Urbnisi belong to the basilica type, as does a very unusual church at Gurjaani in Kakheti, which has two small octagonal domes disposed symmetrically along the top of the edifice. In 1920, the leading Georgian antiquary Ekvtime Taqaishvili made a survey of four remarkable basilican churches in the Qvirila valley, his findings being later published in English in the journal *Georgica* for October, 1936. An interesting basilica at Sioni, high up in the Caucasus near

Plates 37, 40

Figs. 36, 37

Plates 34, 35

Plate 39

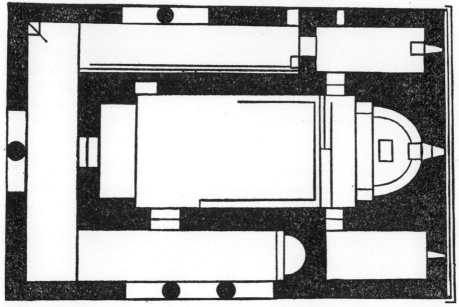

Fig. 37. All Saints' church at Vachnadziani, ground-plan. An interesting ninth-century domed triple basilica in Kakheti province

Mount Kazbek, is illustrated by David Roden Buxton in his *Russian Mediaeval Architecture* (1934).

The next stage in the evolution of Georgian and Armenian ecclesiastical architecture is the cruciform church with central dome, having four principal axial buttresses, and sometimes four lesser ones as well. A unique early variant of this type, which originated in the sixth century, is the ruined episcopal church of Ninodsminda, forty miles east of Tbilisi, the ground plan of which was basically a double quadrilobe, or 8-pointed star. This remarkable building was destroyed in an earthquake in 1825. Among the classic examples of the cruciform church are St Ripsime at Echmiadzin in Armenia, and the Jvari ('Cross') church on top of a steep hill opposite Mtskheta. Jvari is remarkable for its carvings, which extend round most of the

Fig. 38

Plates 36, 38

129

exterior. On the eastern façade we see members of the Iberian ducal family responsible for building and endowing the church, who are shown doing obeisance to Christ, to St Stephen and to the Archangel Michael. These carved figures, in particular the lifelike portrayal of the notables and the detailed representation of their court robes, have been the subject of several mono graphs, the latest being by Vakhtang Jobadze in *Oriens Christi anus* (1960–61). A larger and more elaborate example of this style of church design is the ruined but still impressive edifice at Dsromi, situated near Gomi railway station 100 kilometres west of Tbilisi, and dating from *c.* 630; here a determined effort has been made to improve on the relatively unsophisticated techniques employed at Jvari in a composition on a more grandiose scale. The apse was adorned with a fine mosaic showing Christ standing between two Apostles.

This vital phase in Caucasian church design also witnessed the emergence of a distinctive form of round church, of which good examples are Zvartnotz in Armenia and Bana in the Tao province of south western Georgia, now part of Turkey. With in the circular outer wall, Bana was quadrilobe on the internal ground plan, and of majestic proportions, measuring 38 metres in diameter and 30 metres or more in height. Bana is thought to date from the mid seventh century, and survived until the nineteenth century, when it was used as a fort and shelled in one of the Russo Turkish wars of that period. Only part of the eastern lobe or apse remains standing, to a height of about fifty feet. Another important round church, that of Tavusker (Taos kari), also ruined, dates from the tenth century, and has eight lobes and sixteen exterior facets; it was formerly crowned by a 16 sided central dome with a conical roof.

The onset of full maturity in Georgian church architecture coincides broadly speaking with the establishment and con solidation of Bagratid power in the south western provinces of Tao, Klarjeti and Shavsheti, whence a sense of national revival

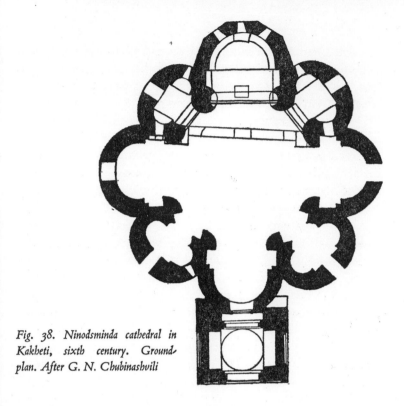

Fig. 38. Ninodsminda cathedral in Kakheti, sixth century. Ground plan. After G. N. Chubinashvili

spread rapidly into Georgia's heartland. The key figures in this renaissance were Ashot Kuropalates (780–826) and his successors, and the militant religious leader St Gregory of Khandzta (759–861), who lived to the age of 102 on a diet of dried cabbage, bread and water. St Gregory's biography, written in 951 by Giorgi Merchule, constitutes a veritable Baedeker to the antiquities of south-western Georgia. We learn how Gregory became the head archimandrite of twelve monasteries in Klarjeti, five of which were built or restored by him, and the others by his disciples. These formed a real monastic republic, with Gregory as their redoubtable president. In some instances, ancient Armenian foundations were taken over and restored. But for the most part the Georgian shrines of Tao-Klarjeti represent fresh foundations, and their architecture marks a new break-through in the evolution of Georgia's distinctive national style of church design, which from now on decidedly parts company with any Armenian prototypes.

These fine churches represent a harmonious combination of the basilica and the centralized church, having what may be described as a choir and a nave, complete with transepts, and a drum-shaped cupola over the crossing, surmounted by a coni-cal roof. A magnificent specimen of this type is the imposing church of Oshki (Öşk Vank), which lies on the left bank of the Tortum River, immediately below Tortum Göl. Built between 958 and 966 by the Eristavi-of-Eristavis Bagrat and the Magistros David, the monastery of Oshki was the greatest in the province of Tao; the church itself is 38 metres long, 36 metres in breadth, and 40 metres high. Its dome is supported on four immense columns, whose massive bases are more than two metres in diameter and two metres high; the drum is decorated with blind arches pierced alternately by round-headed window slits. Oshki is notable for a hexagonal column and capital in a room adjoining the south-western side of the church. This column and capital have miniature figures and stylized foliage carved on them, and are still in good condition. As Mr DavidWinfield remarks, these tenth-century stone carv-ings are of great importance in the history of medieval sculpture, and throw new light on the emergence of the Romanesque style. From the same period dates the cruciform church of Haho (Khakhuli), several miles south of Lake Tortum. Its steep conical roof shines with beautiful red and blue glazed tiles, surmounting a drum of yellow stone, while the rest of the building is of weathered grey blocks. Khakhuli has a number of remarkable archaic reliefs in blackened stone, among them a lion attacking a bull, a great cock, and a crude picture of Jonah being ejected from the whale's mouth. Like several other Georgian churches in Turkey, Khakhuli is kept in a

Plate 50

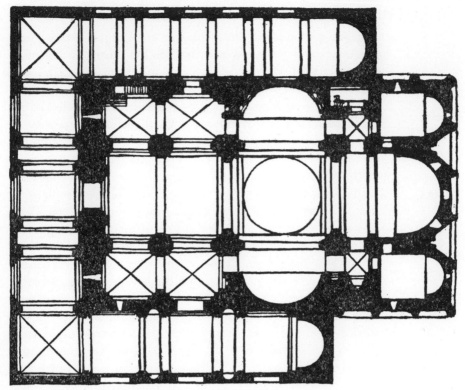

Fig. 39. Allaverdi cathedral, ground-plan. After G. N. Chubinashvili

fair state of preservation by being used as a mosque. Considerable international interest has lately been evinced in this group
of Georgian churches, which have now been extensively
studied by the late Ekvtime Taqaishvili (Georgia), M. and N.
Thierry (France) and Denis Cecil Hills and David Winfield
(Great Britain).

The great unification of the Georgian lands effected under
Bagrat III (975–1014) led to a further burgeoning of architectural genius, manifesting itself in the creation of cathedrals and
monastic ensembles which, in their majestic setting, with the

133

snow-capped peaks of the Caucasus range as a backcloth, can scarcely be matched anywhere in the world. I shall concentrate here on four well-known examples, all of which I myself have visited, namely the ruined Bagrat cathedral at Kutaisi and the near-by monastic centre of Gelati; the cathedral of the Life-Giving Pillar at Mtskheta; and Allaverdi cathedral in the plain of Kakheti. Earliest in date is Bagrat cathedral, completed in 1003, and blown up by the Turks in 1691. Enough of this splendid building has been preserved to permit of its partial restoration, which is proceeding at the present time. In style, this great cruciform, triple-vaulted structure was a logical successor and extension of Oshki and must indeed, to judge from the reconstruction in Irakli Tsitsishvili's handbook of Georgian architecture, have been a building of singular grace and beauty. Numerous carved pillars and capitals scattered around the cathedral grounds, which adjoin one of Kutaisi's main schools, enable us to judge the superb quality of the sculpture of this truly royal foundation. Another Imeretian church of the same period, at Nikordsminda in Ratcha, dating from 1014 and quite well preserved, also has magnificent carvings, which give an excellent idea of the west Georgian stonemasons' craft at this period.

Next in date is the patriarchal cathedral of the Life-Giving Pillar ('Sveti-tskhoveli') in Mtskheta, built by Master Constantine Arsukidze between 1010 and 1029 at the behest of Catholicos-Patriarch Melkisedek. This is the third shrine to occupy the central site of Georgia's ancient Christian capital: first, there was the simple wooden chapel erected by St Nino around AD 330, to be replaced a century and a half later by a basilica erected by King Vakhtang Gorgaslan. Arsukidze's cathedral, itself restored and altered on a number of occasions, is the largest such structure in all Georgia, being 60 metres long, and lofty in proportion. It is unique in that not only the nave, but also the transepts, have a roof of which the slope is

Fig. 39

Plate 45

Plates 46, 47

Fig. 40

Plate 42

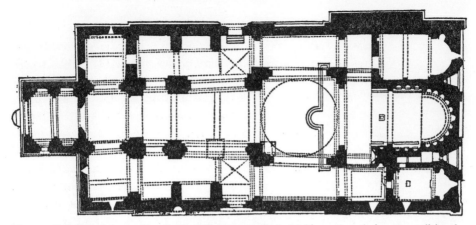

Fig. 40. Cathedral of Sveti-tskhoveli (the Life-Giving Pillar), Mtskheta. Ground-plan. Over-all length 60 m.

interrupted, as in the vaulted basilica. The cathedral walls are arcaded; at the east end, two side arches enclose the recesses marking the position of the apses. The walls are scattered with grotesque beasts carved in stone, while the windows are adorned with imaginative sculpturing, an intertwined vine motif giving especially fine results. A carved representation high up on the north wall of a human hand holding a set-square is tradition-ally held to be that of Master Builder Arsukidze himself, the legend being that the lowly-born architect vied with his sovereign, King Giorgi I, for the love of the duke's daughter Shorena, as a result of which Arsukidze's hand was ordered to be cut off, and Shorena immured in a convent. The whole story of the cathedral and its builder is beautifully told by the Georgian writer Konstantine Gamsakhurdia (b. 1891) in his novel, *The Hand of a Great Master*, an English version of which was published at Moscow in 1959; it has also been turned into an opera by Shalva Mshvelidze. The cathedral stands in a large grass-covered enclosure, surrounded by crenellated walls. Inside are the tombs of Georgian kings and princes right up to the nineteenth century, and interesting historical relics. Also in

Plate 49

the little town of Mtskheta is another striking church of the same period, that of Samtavro, which is notable for its superb stone interlace work surrounding the window apertures.

Plate 43

Plate 53

For the next great monument from the eleventh century, Allaverdi cathedral, we move eastwards to the fertile Alazani valley in Kakheti. Allaverdi has a very tall, attenuated dome, giving it a skyward soaring air which is sublime when viewed against the peaks of Daghestan in the background. It stands amid fields and vineyards, away from human habitation, though within easy driving distance from the remains of Iqalto, one of Georgia's medieval universities, and the former convent of New Shuamta, now an infants' school, perched on a hill amid beech groves. Allaverdi has always been held sacred by Muslim tribesmen from the neighbouring hills, who have a shrine of their own within the cathedral compound. Even in Soviet times, regular pilgrimages and communal feasts are held by the Kakhetian peasantry. Buffaloes and donkeys wander round the peaceful gates, and the visitor may be entertained to a piece of warm *khachapuri* cheese cake and a horn of local wine. The interior is bare, but the fabric is in good structural repair.

Plate 52

An illustrious place in Georgian civilization is occupied by the cathedral, monastery and academy of Gelati, seven miles from the city of Kutaisi. Gelati was constructed and endowed by King David the Builder, who once fell off the scaffolding and was injured. David's full-length fresco portrait, now dis- figured by the illiterate *graffiti* of modern Russian and Georgian tourist parties, still adorns the cathedral wall, as does a splendid mosaic in the apse showing the Virgin and Child with Arch- angels Michael and Gabriel, this being the gift of the Byzantine emperor. The ensemble includes three domed churches, com- pleted between 1106 and 1125, the main cathedral being dedi- cated to the Virgin Mary, and the smaller chapels, one being perched above a well, to St George and St Nicholas respec- tively. The proportions of the cathedral, with its three projecting eastern apses, are extremely dignified and satisfying, and gain much from the expanse of greensward over which the various buildings are deployed. The choice of situation, on a pleasant wooded hill above the River Dsqaldsitela, within sight of the main Caucasus range, adds to the general impression of the whole, which must be numbered among the gems of world architecture. A colour film about the monastery, the sound/track including hymns and chants of the Georgian medieval Church, was shown with success during the International Congress of Orientalists held in Moscow in 1960.

Though we have not carried this brief survey of Georgian ecclesiastical architecture beyond the twelfth century, there are many churches of pleasing proportions and rich ornamental carving which date from the thirteenth and later centuries; but these are usually mere variants on well/established prototypes. Georgia's contribution to world architecture, particularly to the development of the Romanesque style throughout the Byzan/tine and Mediterranean world has been greatly underesti/mated, chiefly through the inability of historians of architecture to distinguish between the Georgian and Armenian styles which, though often similar in outline and ground/plan, differ considerably in carved ornament, in contour and proportions, in disposition of the altar, and in a host of other particulars. The Armenians were fond of angular, purely geometrical patterns (which they applied with equal skill to the surrounds of church windows and doors, or to the fine silver ware for which they are still renowned in the East), whereas the Geor/gians favoured a much more sinuous, rounded interlace, in Plates 48, 49, 51 association with a leaf/like 'palmette' ornamental motif. Armenian taste in stone carving, which has close affinities with that of Islam, is given fullest expression in the memorial stone *hachkar*, a universal adjunct to all Armenian churches, but absent in Georgia. A contributory cause of the relative neglect of Georgian church architecture arises from the individual,

rather fanciful theories of the Viennese art historian Josef Strzygowski, who claimed that virtually all Christian architecture,
including that of Constantinople, the Balkans and Romanesque Europe, derived from ancient, sometimes vanished
Armenian models. As the Georgians did not fit into his
scheme, Strzygowski virtually ignored them. The work of
modern English scholars, such as David Roden Buxton, and
David and Tamara Talbot Rice, has done much to redress the
balance.

A certain amount of nonsense has been talked about the
alleged 'atectonic' quality of Georgian and Armenian buildings. According to Jurgis Baltrušaitis, these Caucasian
churches suffer from the fact that the outside form conceals
rather than brings out the complex design of the interior.
Detail is spread like a garment over the blank surface of exterior walls, without relation to the 'tectonics' of the edifice,
whereas it should be the architect's duty to relate the external
outline and decoration of a building to its internal structural
mechanics. From this, Baltrušaitis argues that Georgian and
Armenian master builders were geometricians, masons, decora-
tors, but not architects in the highest sense of the term. 'In the
Romanesque churches ornament is subsidiary to structure, is
used in conjunction with structure, and serves to emphasize it.
In Transcaucasia, on the contrary, ornament is independent,
and serves rather to mask the structure of the building than to
express it.' This line of reasoning appears extremely arbitrary
and hypothetical, especially as these ancient Caucasian churches
give an impression of grace combined with monumentality
seldom surpassed anywhere in the world. As for mastery of the
mechanical and engineering side of construction—one might as
well argue that the structurally essential, if aesthetically irrelevant device of the flying buttress, without which many Gothic
cathedrals could scarcely stand upright, detracts from the merit
of the great medieval architects of France, Germany and Eng-

land. We may also recall that the annals of medieval Christendom are full of accounts of Gothic towers and steeples collapsing of their own weight upon the unsuspecting faithful. Georgian and Armenian churches, on the other hand, have survived centuries of neglect and pillage, earthquake and bombardment, and yet hundreds still stand erect as witnesses to the solid handi/work of Caucasian masons of that by/gone Golden Age.

Among the features on which special care was lavished were the archivolts and tympana above church doors, where the carving (*chukurtma*) is often uncommonly fine. There are some magnificent doors in carved wood still surviving, particularly in upland Svaneti, which can be assigned to the tenth and eleventh centuries. Inside, churches such as Sapara, Shio/Mghwime, Katskhi and many others were equipped with splendid stone altar/partitions or iconostases. In medieval churches, these partitions were always low and open, so that the congregation could see all that was displayed on the altar and all that was proceeding in the chancel during Divine Service. The iconostasis was usually in the form of a low wall of stone slabs, rising two steps above the floor, with a space in the centre for a door; set upon the wall were columns or pilasters with cornice, forming an arch, but not blocking the congrega/gation's view. The ancient altar partitions are mostly of cut stone, ornamented with beautiful figures of saints, Biblical scenes, and exquisitely executed Georgian interlacing. From the fifteenth century onwards, we find iconostases of alabaster, or stone/faced cement or alabaster stucco, decorated with arab/esques in polychrome or fresco paintings of saints. High, closed iconostases, with several levels, begin to appear in the seven/teenth century, and spread considerably in the eighteenth cen/tury and after the Russian annexation; many of these are hideous in the extreme. Of special historical interest is what remains of the seventh/century iconostasis from Tsebelda in Abkhazia, portraying scenes from the life of St Eustace Placidus, and the

Plate 36

Plates 58, 59

quaint altar-partition from the Shio-Mghwime Lavra, depicting St Shio himself wearing a high peaked hood, the dove
which brought him food in its beak, together with a local
knight, Evagrius (later Shio's disciple), mounted on a horse
of Georgian breed and wearing a high hat. These ancient altar-
partitions were unfortunately among the first targets of vandals
during the Revolution, and little of them has survived.

Equally sad is the fate of Georgia's truly magnificent frescoes. Many of these, such as those in Sveti-Tskhoveli cathedral
at Mtskheta, were whitewashed by Russian prelates in the
nineteenth century and can be uncovered with a little care.
Irreparably damaged, on the other hand, are those in churches
whose roofs let in the damp, or where Georgian tourists who
should know better seek to immortalize themselves by carving
their names all over wondrous paintings of angels, saints, and
even of Georgia's own ancient kings and heroes. Fortunately
there now exists an influential society for the preservation of
cultural monuments, which is having some success in curbing
vandalism of various kinds. Georgian frescoes are far more than
slavish imitations of Byzantine models. In the case of such
gems as Qindsvisi, Ateni, or the little church at Ubisi, lov-
Plates 60, 61, 54 ingly studied and recorded by Shalva Amiranashvili, the
Georgian artists enrich their subject with countless original
touches, often highly naturalistic. Far from reproducing stiff
and stereotyped Greek saints, the Georgians endow their paintings with movement and grace; here, we see a nobleman holding in his hand the model of a church which he has built;
there, a king and his family paying homage to Jesus Christ.
Even in the faces of Biblical figures, the Georgians did not
hesitate to paint in the physical traits of their own nation, so
that it is hard to tell whether we are looking at Abraham or
Moses, or the venerable chief of some ancient Georgian tribe.
Now that Balkan and Russian frescoes are studied and appre-
ciated for their own sake, it will not be long before Georgian

fresco painting—or what the Georgians succeed in rescuing of it—comes in for its own meed of discriminating praise.

One branch of medieval art in which the Georgians' con-Plates 62–70 tribution is not disputed is that of repoussé work, cloisonné enamels, and the craft of the gold- and silversmith generally. Between the tenth and thirteenth centuries, Georgian craftsmen produced masterpieces ranking with the best of contemporary Byzantium or Italy. The genres in which they excelled were connected with the practice and cult of Christianity—pectoral and processional crosses, chalices, jewelled covers for illum- inated Gospel manuscripts, reliquaries—above all, frames, holders and settings for icons. Regal insignia, gold plate and other secular items also existed in abundance in the palaces of Georgia's kings and queens, but these were mostly looted and destroyed in the successive sackings of Georgian cities which occurred throughout the Middle Ages.

Two great masters are known to us by name—Beka and Beshken Opizari—so designated after the monastic centre of Opiza in Klarjeti, where they plied their craft with distinction during the late twelfth and early thirteenth centuries. One of Beka's masterpieces is the icon of Anchi, preserved in the Tbilisi State Museum of Art along with other breath-taking examples of Georgian artistry in repoussé work, cloisonné enamel and other products of the goldsmith's art. Beka and Beshken were unquestionably responsible for many other master works, to some of which they omitted to sign their name, while others have perished. Apart from Opiza, flourishing centres of craftsmanship in precious metals and gems existed at Tbeti and at the monastery and academy of Gelati. The Gelati school is famed for the wondrous Khakhuli triptych in gold, precious Plate 69 stones and enamels, made by three unknown masters during the reign of Dimitri I (1125–54) to enshrine the miracle- working image of Our Lady of Khakhuli, which had been removed for safety from its original home in south-western

Georgia when this area was overrun by the Seljuk Turks. The Khakhuli triptych, which has been compared to the Pala d'Oro at St Mark's, Venice, had a chequered history, the magnificent enamelled icon of the Virgin being detached in the nineteenth century and sold to a Russian collector with the connivance of the governor of Kutaisi, Count Levashov. The work has now been reassembled (though the central icon remains fragmentary), and is on view in Georgia.

The colourful cloisonné enamel medallions and miniatures inset on many of these gold icons are of both Georgian and Greek workmanship. In some instances, enamelled medallions would be detached from damaged or worn-out presentation objects sent from Constantinople by the Byzantine emperors, and re-used by Georgian goldsmiths in subsequent creations; hence dating is sometimes difficult. A sumptuously produced album, *Les Emaux de Géorgie*, by the director of the Georgian State Museum of Art at Tbilisi, Professor Shalva Amiranashvili, was published in Paris in 1962, so that Western connoisseurs can fully appreciate the quality of these superb examples of medieval craftsmanship.

A minor art which flourished in Georgia, particularly at the town of Dmanisi, between the eleventh and thirteenth centuries was that of decorative coloured pottery, on which research has been done by the Soviet scholars V. Japaridze and Z. Maisuradze, and by the American art historian Jay D. Frierman in Los Angeles. Dmanisi was an important trading centre about 100 kilometres south-west of Tbilisi; coins were struck at Dmanisi in 1244–45, and the city had close connections with the trading cities of Iran, which helps to explain some of the favourite motifs employed by the Dmanisi potters. Very attractive designs and patterns were given to this Dmanisi ware by means of an *engobe* or coloured wash finish, with a high gloss. In Frierman's view, a comparison of Georgian pottery with contemporary Armenian work 'simply proves the artistic originality of the Georgian potters. However, it would appear that the Armenians are technically more advanced in that they produced faïence, while the Georgians do not seem to have perfected this type of material.'

Jay D. Frierman has specially drafted for inclusion in this book the following notes on Georgian pottery of the eleventh to the thirteenth century, based in part on specimens in his own collection:

'In a culturally peripheral region, existing in an atmosphere of intense pressure generated by its powerful neighbors, one can only expect a style of eclectic compromise. Yet this very eclecticism represents a volitional choice. In architecture, paint‐ing and manuscript illumination the choice was Byzantium and the West. However, neither Byzantium nor the West had a great ceramic culture and it was Islam (especially Seljuk Iran) that supplied the style and technique for the Medieval Geor‐gian ceramics. The factor of religion played no great part. To be sure, Byzantine and Chersonese designs (crosses for instance) appear, but no more frequently than they do in Egypt or Iran. There is one factor of the greatest importance and that is the ceramics of China of the T'ang, the Five Dynasties and the Sung. Chinese ceramics have been found at several archaeologi‐cal sites in Transcaucasia.

'The potters of Georgia shared with their Muslim peers that profound admiration for Chinese ceramics that has been the major influence on Islam since the ninth century. Out of this protean milieu was produced the ceramic culture of medieval Georgia.

'Georgian ceramics are technically akin to Iranian wares. They are usually thrown on the wheel and fired in domed, bee‐hive kilns. In these kilns the fire box is directly beneath the chamber and communicates with it by way of a system of flues. The firing temperature and atmosphere were well controlled, the wares being evenly and thoroughly fired. With the

exception of *lustre* wares all the pottery was fired in an oxidiz-
ing atmosphere. Complete collections of potter's equipment,
kiln furniture and kilns have been found at Tbilisi, Dmanisi,
Gudarekhi, Rustavi, Iqalto, etc.

'During the medieval period three distinct types of wares
were produced:

1. A coarse pottery with a fine *lies de vin* engobe that was
used exclusively for unglazed wares. These include such vessels
as tall ewers, wide-mouth two-handle pots and the small,
spherical to conical, narrow-mouth vessels which are variously
described as "grenades", "perfume", or "mercury" bottles.
The impressed relief ornaments include pairs of confronted
birds, dogs or wolves, goats and incised "cypress" trees, as well
as various simple geometric motifs. In all these works are strong
reminiscences of the red-glazed, relief-decorated *terra sigillata* of
Roman times. These wares come to their Classic ancestry by
way of Sasanian and Byzantine ancestors and are among the
last of their types.

2. The pink-buff earthenware bodies that are characteristic
of the bulk of the glazed pottery. These clays are variable in both
color and texture, tending to be rather coarse. To prevent the
body color from discoloring the transparent glazes a pure, white
engobe is used under the glazed portions of the pots.

'The Georgian glazed ceramics are of great importance
because they are among the few medieval ceramic cultures that
have been scientifically excavated and have been found in
connection with their kilns. Spectographic analysis has indi-
cated an unexpected variety and technical sophistication of the
glaze formulations. Glazes very similar in appearance can be
high lead-sodium alkali-silicate or lead-free alkali-silicates and
anything in between. Thus, in Georgia, the alkali-silicate
glazes of the faïences seem to have been in existence prior to the
production of these wares. These glazes are brilliant, transparent
and beautiful. The principal colors are blue, turquoise and

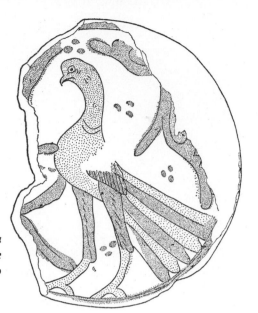

Fig. 41. Bird of prey, in brown and green on a piece of a shallow bowl of glazed pottery in the State Museum of Georgia, Tbilisi. Twelfth century. 17·5 × 13·0 cm. After Japaridze.

green, all derived from copper; aubergine from manganese; yellow, brown and orange from iron.

'The glazed earthenwares date from the last quarter of the eleventh century to the first third of the thirteenth century. Stylistically the majority must be assigned to the first half of this period.

'The glazed wares are primarily thick, shallow bowls and various vases. All of these have ring bases. The bowls tend to be less steep-sided and shallower than similar Iranian vessels. There is also a group of small shallow bowls with various types of flanged lips which are referred to as "salts". There are two principal types of vases—the Islamic *alberello* and a shoulder vase whose shape and ornament indicate a Chinese ancestry. The ornament, shape and color are all "Chinese". The shape seems closest to certain *yüeh yao* vases of the tenth century and the ornament seems identical in repertory and placement to the well-known *mei-p'ing* vases of the Sung.

Fig. 42. Lion, in green and brown, on a shallow bowl of pottery from Kaspi, Kartli province, in the State Museum of Georgia. Twelfth century, Diameter: 21·9 cm. After Japaridze

'The most interesting of all the Georgian ceramics are the T'ang-inspired polychrome glazed earthenwares. Where true splashed wares are rare in Georgia, designs rendered in green, yellow, and brown on white engobe or turquoise, green, blue and cerise on a pink engobe are common. The latter combination is uniquely Georgian.

Fig. 43. 'Sun face' motif, in yellow and brown, on a fragment of a bowl of glazed pottery from Dmanisi. Twelfth century. 9·2 ×8·6 cm. After V. V. Japaridze

Fig. 44. Decorative line and spiral pattern in blue, yellow, green and brown on a shallow bowl of glazed pottery in the Tbilisi Historical and Ethnographic Museum. Twelfth century. Diameter: 18·4 cm. After Japaridze

'The lively designs include besides the ubiquitous birds of prey ("eagles"), lions, rabbits, goats, tigers, and a wolf or dog-like animal. Besides animals a few human representations occur. These include a unique motif of a sun-like face in the center of a bowl; R. Ghirshman remarks that "... these faces are a revival of the Proto-Iranian motif of 'heads cut short at the chin' (Cemetery B, Sialk) which so often figure in Luristan bronzes ... Henceforth they had a considerable vogue throughout the Roman world, in South Russia and even Siberia."

Figs. 41, 42

Fig. 43

'There are also a number of medallion bowls wholly reminiscent of the T'ang although of greater simplicity. The motif is, of course, originally derived from Sasanian metal work. Equally remarkable are the group of bowls with their centers filled with over-all patterns of quatrefoils, hour glasses, and checker boards. All of these motifs are known in Iran during the fourth millennium BC and for several millennia thereafter. Their unique reappearance in Georgia at this time is extremely difficult to explain.

Fig. 44

3. The synthetic faïence bodies which are an apparent redis-covery of an Egyptian and Near Eastern artificial body. This type of ware seemingly disappears in Early Islamic times only to reappear again at the end of the twelfth century. This body consists of ground quartz plasticized by the addition of a small quantity of white firing bentonite (a clay of volcanic origin, montmorillonite) and an equal quantity of a frit that has a composition that is duplicated by the alkali-silicate glaze. Faïence bodies must be glazed with alkali-silicate glazes as lead glazes do not adhere well. This material when fired produces a pure white, gritty body that is slightly translucent in its thinnest sections where the glaze can flux the body.

'A small number of faïences have been found. These include monochrome vessels in ultramarine blue and turquoise, *lustre* ware and over-painted tin glazes. The most typically local of these wares are faïences with reliefs of human heads and daisy-like flowers. These seem to be especially common in Armenia and may well be a Transcaucasian innovation.

'The over-painted (enamelled) tin glazed wares are best represented by the handsome floor of hexagonal and rhomboid tiles before the altar in the church of Ozaani. This monument is dated to the end of the eleventh or alternatively the early twelfth century.

'The *lustres* seem closest to those of Rayy. The figures and designs are in a brownish or greenish gold and occasionally black or blue are added. A handsome vase fragment of appar-ently local inspiration has gold spirals on an intense ultra-marine ground. Japaridze suggests that all the lustre wares are Iranian imports, and probably from Sultanabad.

'In one way or another, virtually all the glazed ceramics of Georgia owe something to the Chinese ceramics of the T'ang and the Sung. The desire to produce a ware comparable to the imported Chinese products seemed to be an almost universal obsession with the potters of Islam and those regions, such as

Georgia, that although Christian, partook of a good deal of Islamic culture.

'The eclectic nature of Georgian ceramics is readily apparent in technique and in style, yet there is on the whole a remarkable uniqueness that seems in complete contradiction to the provincial eclecticism of the culture. Unlike a true folk culture, Georgia does not develop a style outside the mainstreams of Middle Eastern art but rather adds a charming and original rusticity to the myriad forms of the great medieval ceramics of Iran, Byzantium and China.'

In conclusion, we must not forget that Georgia has a rich and ancient musical culture. After a banquet, Georgians launch spontaneously into remarkable polyphonic drinking songs. These are closely connected with the country's ecclesiastical chants of the medieval period. An eleventh-century source speaks of the existence in Byzantium and Georgia of two kinds of vocal music—the Greek and the Georgian—the former being homophonic, the latter sung in three voices. From ancient times, Georgia's neighbours had known only of homophonic chant, so that Georgian music, with its developed polyphony, both in folk songs and church music, and its original harmonization, was an exception to the environment, a kind of island in a sea of homophony. Ancient sources point out that whenever the texts of hymns were translated from Greek into Georgian, the accompanying music was written anew, for as a twelfth-century Georgian author observed, 'alien to our people are the Greek canticles'. Among the most eminent composers of hymns were St Gregory of Khandzta (759–861), and Michael Modrekili and Ioane Mtbevari in the tenth century.

The musical notations on manuscripts of ancient Georgian liturgies remained long undeciphered. Nine principal manuscripts, several beautifully illuminated, containing specimens of ancient Georgian musical notations or neumes survive—five in Georgia, one on Mount Athos, and three in the library of

St Catharine's monastery on Mount Sinai. A Georgian philo-
logist, Pavle Ingoroqva, succeeded in reconstructing the actual
melodies of these ecclesiastical chants. Commenting on
Ingoroqva's article published in English in the *UNESCO
Courier* for May, 1962, Dr Egon Wellesz, the leading authority
on Byzantine music, wrote in a letter to me: 'The neumes
reproduced by Ingoroqva are those which P. Aubry and J.-B.
Thibaut found and studied half a century ago (and I ten years
later) in *Armenian* MSS. The red signs are usually signs for the
execution. Similar signs occur in tenth- and eleventh-century
Byzantine MSS. They are interval signs, I should say signs
indicating the rise and fall of a melody which the singer knows
by heart . . . The author has rediscovered the metric system of
Orthodox hymnography which J.-B. Pitra stated in 1867, but
it is strange that he did not study the Armenian neumes.' None
the less, there can be no doubt that Ingoroqva's researches constitute an important contribution to the study of Georgian
hymnography, in relation to that of Byzantium, Russia and
Armenia.

The medieval Georgians greatly enjoyed instrumental music,
religious and secular. Manuscript illustrations show that they
performed on cymbals, the lute, the tabor and the flute. One
striking Georgian medieval miniature shows Gideon and his
Israelite band giving a spirited performance on Caucasian
trumpets, putting the Midianites effectively to flight. On the
occasion of Queen Tamar's marriage to David Soslan in 1189,
a musical performance or *sakhioba* was given, with the participa-
tion of numerous minstrels (*mgosani*) and acrobats, as well as
displays of knightly prowess. The peasants of Guria and Mingrelia are expert performers on the pan-pipes (*lartchemi*);
Valentina Steshenko-Kuftina wrote a most interesting monograph on these Georgian pan-pipes, citing parallels from
ancient Greece and Asia Minor, as well as South America,
China, and South East Asia. Other favourite wind instru-

Fig. 45. Ancient stringed instruments from Abkhazia: Left, the ayumaa; *right, the* akhymaa

ments are the *stviri* or bagpipes, the *salamuri* pipe (there was once a satirical paper entitled 'The Whip and the *Salamuri*'), and the *duduki*, a sort of clarinet, whence the refrain, 'I love wine, the *duduki*, and the girls.' Favourite stringed instruments include the *chonguri*, a kind of mandoline with silk strings, as well as several types of primitive lyre.

Fig. 45

Modern Georgian composers, such as Zakaria Paliashvili (1872–1933) and Dimitri Araqishvili (1873–1953) have drawn freely on this heritage for their operas, the glory of the Georgian State Theatre of Opera and Ballet, itself renowned throughout the Soviet Union.

CHAPTER VII

Literature and Learning

LONG BEFORE THE GEORGIANS possessed their own alphabet and literature, they were versed in the learning and lore of the Greek and Iranian worlds, as well as having legends passed down by word of mouth. Ancient sources contain references to centres of higher education in Colchis, organized on the Greek model, while pious writers of the Middle Ages make it clear that a holocaust of Zoroastrian books took place when Georgia was converted by St Nino in the fourth century. Records of the Byzantine and Persian campaigns in Lazica during the sixth century speak of state archives containing treaties between the Lazic kings and neighbouring powers, doubtless written in Greek.

A major break-through in our knowledge of writing and epigraphy in pre-Christian Georgia occurred in 1940, when two stone slabs with inscriptions were discovered not far from Mtskheta. One of these was a bilingual epitaph of a Georgian princess named Serapita, with closely corresponding though not quite identical texts in Greek and Middle Persian, the latter written in an unusual form of Aramaic which has been called the Armazi script. Deciphered and published in 1942 by Professor Giorgi Tsereteli, Serapita's epitaph, dating from about AD 150, is touching in its restrained dignity and pathos, and deserves to rank as the most ancient connected literary text from Georgia:

Plate 29

> I am Serapita, daughter of Zevakh the younger, *pitiakhsh* [chief minister, viceroy] of Farsman the king, and wife of Iodmangan the victorious, winner of many conquests, master of the court of Ksefarnug, the great king of the Iberians, and son of Agrippa, master of the court of King Farsman. Woe,

woe, for the sake of her who was not of full age, whose years were not completed, and so good and beautiful that no one was like her in excellence; and she died at the age of twenty-one.

Though the date and circumstances of the invention of the Georgian alphabet have often been disputed, the facts seem incontrovertible. Christianity, we know, became the official religion of Armenia and Iberia early in the fourth century, and also spread rapidly into neighbouring Caucasian Albania. After a century of worship from Greek and Syriac texts, the need for religious books in the vernacular became pressing throughout Christian Caucasia. With the encouragement of the Byzantine Church, a commission was set up under St Mesrop (Mashtotz), a leading Armenian cleric, who worked with local informants and produced amazingly precise phonetic tables of the sounds in the Armenian, Georgian and Albanian languages. On the basis of these, but following where applicable the general order of the Greek alphabet, systems of writing were evolved for all three Christian nations and put into use early in the fifth century. The inventors of these outstandingly accurate and elegant alphabets tried to reproduce as far as possible the appearance of contemporary Greek uncials; comparison of a page of the Codex Sinaiticus or Codex Alexandrinus with the oldest known Georgian or Armenian inscriptions and codices makes this immediately evident. It also seems that account was taken of the distinctive Armazi variety of Aramaic script featuring on Serapita's epitaph and one or two other inscriptions, though Georgian writing, unlike Aramaic, runs from left to right, and represents generally speaking a complete break with Georgia's pagan past.

Once equipped with an alphabet of their own, the Georgians set rapidly to work to adorn public buildings with carved inscriptions, and to evolve a literature both original and in

Fig. 46. Inscription of Abba Antoni, from a mosaic floor at the Georgian monastery near Bethlehem, c. AD 550. One of three ancient inscriptions, from AD 440 onwards, and among the oldest known examples of Georgian ecclesiastical script

Plate 33

Fig. 46

translation. The monumental carved *khutsuri* inscription on Bolnisi Sioni cathedral in Kartli province dates from 492–493, and the mosaics from the Georgian cloister near Bethlehem are somewhat earlier. From Armenian, the Georgians soon trans-lated the Four Gospels and Psalms of David, to be followed by other Biblical and liturgical texts. Many of these early re-dactions, which go back in some instances to lost Syriac and Greek originals, are exceptionally interesting and preserve readings not witnessed elsewhere. In the Passion of St Eustace the Cobbler, put to death by the Persian governor of Tbilisi in 545, we find a curious formulation of the Ten Command-ments, and an account of the Life of Christ which recalls Tatian's *Diatessaron*, a Gospel harmony of the second century, and suggests that the Georgian Church in early times possessed a *Diatessaron* of its own. The apologia of Archdeacon Samuel in this Passion of St Eustace is of great value, as showing how the Christian faith was expounded among Persian and Geor-gian Christians in Sasanian times.

Pride of place among the first original works of Georgian literature belongs to the Passion of St Shushanik, composed by the martyr's father-confessor Jacob of Tsurtavi between 476 and 483. The background of the saint's life is well known from historical sources. Shushanik's father, Vardan Mamikonian, was the hero of the Armenian national rising of 451 directed against the Sasanian monarch Yezdegird of Iran. Shushanik married the Georgian duke Varsken, lord of Tsurtavi, a strategic castle on the frontier between Armenia and Georgia. Varsken became an apostate, abandoning Christianity for Mazdaism to ingratiate himself with the Persian court. Shushanik's refusal to follow him in this step infuriated her ambitious husband, who tortured and humiliated her for seven years, until she finally succumbed and died. (See Chapter V, p. 98.)

Jacob Tsurtaveli's treatment of this tragic and dramatic theme is highly effective, with its thorough mastery of the narrative form, vivid characterization, and use of realistic detail. The proud and high-born Armenian lady, her drunken scoundrel of a Georgian husband, his good-natured but rather ineffective brother, who intercedes for Shushanik, but cannot prevent the final tragedy—these characters come to life as creatures of flesh and blood. The secondary figures, such as Varsken's Persian factotum, an oily hypocrite with a wheedling, lachrymose voice, are also infused with this lifelike quality, which makes itself felt in numerous details, as when a junior deacon tries to encourage the tormented Shushanik. 'He attempted to cry out: "Stand fast!", when Varsken cast his eye upon him. He just managed to call out: "Sta . . .", and then was silent and hastily took to his heels and ran away.' This text is important both for the study of political and social relationships and religious conflicts in fifth-century Georgia, and for its realistic description of everyday life. The health and hygiene of dwellers in that low-lying region of the Mtkvari valley are described in lurid terms. 'In the summer time, the heat of the sun burns like fire, the winds are torrid and the waters infected. The inhabitants of this region are themselves afflicted with various diseases, being swollen with dropsy, yellow with jaundice, pock-marked, withered up, mangy, pimply, bloated of face and brief of life, and nobody attains to old age in that district.'

This vivid realism, combined with patriotic and religious fervour, is also in evidence in the Passion of St Abo, a per-fumer from Baghdad, put to death by the Arab governor of Tbilisi in 786. His life was written by a Georgian contempo-rary, Ioane Sabanisdze, partly to inspire his own countrymen to further efforts through the heroic example of this Arab stranger who chose martyrdom for the sake of Georgia's own Christian faith. Abo's Passion is impregnated with the simple unquestioning faith of early Christianity, and contains valuable historical data, including an account of the Turkic Khazars who lived by the Volga, and were visited by St Abo during his travels.

A different, though equally interesting group of hagio-graphical documents are concerned with the lives of early Georgian hermits, monks and anchorites. These are no dry chronicles of monastic trivialities; they breathe a warm, human spirit, and are characteristically Georgian in their sympathetic treatment of human foibles. One readable collection, known as the *Lives of the Syrian Fathers*, was compiled and revised by Catholicos Arsenius II of Georgia between 955 and 980. These Syrian Fathers, thirteen in number, arrived in the Cau-casus at various times between the end of the fifth and the middle of the sixth century, and brought with them the rules and pre-cepts of Syrian and Egyptian monasticism, which they helped to implant in Georgia.

Hermits though they were, the Syrian Fathers were by no means misanthropic in outlook. St Iese of Dsilkani, for in-stance, obliged his parishioners by diverting the River Ksani to flow through their town. Several of the Fathers were distin-guished by love of animals. Ioane Zedazneli made friends with bears near his hermitage, while St Shio employed a tame wolf to guide the donkeys which brought supplies to his lonely grotto. St David of Garesja and his disciple Lucian in their desert abode in Outer Kakheti received milk and curds from three tame deer. The cellar of their cave was infested by a fearsome dragon with bloodshot eyes, a horn growing out of his forehead, and a great mane on his neck. Eventually God sends a thunderbolt which burns the dragon to a cinder. St David—and this is another typically Georgian touch—protests vigorously to Heaven against this violence to one of his own protégés, and has to be pacified by an angel sent specially by the Almighty Himself.

Endearing touches are found too in the Life of St Gregory of Khandzta by Giorgi Merchule, written in 951, in which we read of a Bishop Zacharias, who was annoyed by a blackbird persistently pecking at his ripe grape-vine. Zacharias makes the sign of the cross over the bird, which immediately falls dead; repenting of his severity, the bishop makes the sign of the cross once more, and the blackbird revives and flies off to its nest. A discerning reader can extract from these *Vitae* countless facts about daily life in medieval Georgia. Sometimes it is necessary to read between the lines, as in the Life of St Serapion of Zarzma, where the monkish biographer's criticism of a hostile peasantry discloses the existence of resentment among the poor farmers at the prosperity of the monasteries, which monopolized the best land and conveniently forgot their vow of poverty.

The beginnings of Georgian historical writing are themselves connected with stories of early saints, as well as containing accounts of the origin of mankind deriving from the Book of Genesis and other conventional sources. The earliest Georgian chronicle, known as the *Conversion of Iberia*, was composed in the seventh century and preserved in the Shatberdi codex copied in 973–976; it centres on the mission of St Nino and the events which attended the adoption of Christianity in Georgia in the fourth century. Between 790 and 900, Juansher Juansheriani wrote a History of King Vakhtang Gorgaslan.

These ancient historical works are valuable for their information, both authentic and legendary, about Georgia's early history, and for their echoes of Iranian and Armenian heroic tradition.

Another group of Georgian histories dates from the eleventh century, when Sumbat son of David composed a history and genealogy of the Bagration house, in which he attempts to establish their descent from David and Solomon of Israel. Probably about the same time, Leonti Mroveli (archbishop of Ruisi) composed a *History of the First Fathers and Kings*, dealing with the era of Georgian history prior to the fifth century. Differences of opinion still exist concerning the epoch and identity of Leonti Mroveli, a central figure in Georgian historiography. Lively interest was aroused by the discovery in 1957 of a secret refuge in the Trekhvi caves, built during the Seljuk invasions, and having a dated inscription running:

'I, Leonti Mroveli, with great labour built this cave for the icon of the Lord God and against adverse times, to provide shelter for the children [*i.e.* the Chapter] of Ruisi cathedral in the time of desolation wrought by the Sultan Alp-Arslan, in the 286th Koronikon (= AD 1066)'.

This inscription, published with commentary and illustrations by Givi Gaprindashvili in the Bulletin of the Social Sciences Department of the Georgian Academy in 1961, provides weighty evidence in favour of placing Leonti Mroveli and his writings in the eleventh rather than in the eighth century. In spite of this, Professor Cyril Toumanoff and one or two others persist in regarding Leonti Mroveli as an eighth-century author. It is, of course, possible that Ruisi was blessed with two outstanding archbishops, both named Leonti, with a gap of three centuries between them, but it seems for the time being more logical to identify Leonti the historian with Leonti of the Trekhvi caves, who flourished around 1066, during the reign of King Bagrat IV of Georgia (1027–72).

The chronicles of Leonti, Sumbat and Juansher helped to form the nucleus of the vast official corpus of Georgian history, known as *Kartlis tskhovreba*, or 'The Life of Georgia'. As time went by, new works were added to keep the corpus up to date. The final revision was made by King Vakhtang VI early in the eighteenth century, and separate histories of the individual king, doms and principalities were composed later in the same cen, tury by Vakhtang's natural son, Prince Vakhushti (1695–1772).

Meanwhile, Georgian literature became further enriched by contact with the treasury of early Christian and Patristic literature. Georgian monks founded cloisters and libraries in all the main centres of the Christian East, including Palestine, Mount Sinai, the Black Mountain near Antioch, Cyprus, and also, Mount Olympus, Mount Athos, and Bachkovo (Petrit, soni) in Bulgaria. As early as 440, Peter the Iberian, a rich and pious scion of the Georgian royal house, was building pilgrim hostels and monasteries in Jerusalem and the Judaean desert near Bethlehem. Peter the Iberian was later prominent in the monophysite cause, in opposition to the canons of the Council of Chalcedon (451). It is this Peter, regarded as one of the most formidable theologians of his time, who has since been identi, fied by the late Ernest Honigmann and by Shalva Nutsubidze as author of the spiritual writings known as the works of 'Dionysius the Areopagite'.

Many important works of eastern literature and wisdom reached the Georgians through direct translation from Arabic. Most readable of these is the story of Barlaam and Josaphat, known in Georgian as *Balavariani*, or *The Wisdom of Balahvar*. This book contains, in modified form, an account of the con, version of Gautama Buddha, the Bodhisattva prince, his Great Renunciation and his missionary journeys. It was popular among the Manichaeans of Central Asia, who transmitted it to the Arabic literary world of Baghdad; it was then translated into Georgian in the ninth century. It is an epitome of all the arguments in favour of the ascetic life and rejection of the joys of this world. The Georgian version was rendered into Greek by St Euthymius the Athonite (955–1028), and then from Greek into Latin and thence into the main languages of medieval Christendom.

The scene of the Georgian *Balavariani* or Barlaam and Josa-phat legend is set in India, at the court of King Abenes of Sulabat, corresponding to King Suddhodana of Kapilavastu, the historical father of the Buddha. Abenes is sorrowful be-cause he has no son and heir. Through divine intervention, a baby boy is eventually born to his consort, and is given the name Iodasaph (or Budhasaf, *i.e.* the Bodhisattva). An astrologer pre-dicts, as in the Buddha life stories, that the glory which the royal child would attain is not of this world below, but that he would be a great guide upon the road to truth. According to the Indian *Jataka* tales, this prediction was made by a Brah-min, who foretold that the prince would forsake the world after witnessing Four Omens, that is to say, a man worn out by age, a sick man, a dead body, and a monk. In both Indian and Christian versions, the king takes stringent precautions against the young prince becoming aware of the frailty of human life; the boy is shut up in a luxurious palace, and whenever he rides out, the streets are cleared of all cripples, mendicants and monks. However, the king is powerless to prevent his son from awakening to knowledge of the truth of life and death, and the Omens one by one are all fulfilled. The king embarks on a fierce persecution of all ascetics and Christian believers, while trying to distract the prince and attach him to the world by all manner of worldly temptations and sexual allurements.

At this point in the Georgian Barlaam and Josaphat (*Bala-variani*) legend, a holy hermit named Balahvar (Barlaam) arrives from Ceylon on a divine mission to reveal to Prince Iodasaph (Josaphat) the way to everlasting salvation. He preaches to him a series of lengthy sermons, reproducing quite closely the ancient Buddhist doctrines of the impermanence of the World, the impurity of the human body, the worthlessness of human existence, the conquest of sin, and the life of the hereafter. Conveniently ignoring the opposite and equally cogent argument, namely, 'Eat, drink and be merry, for to' morrow we die,' Balahvar draws a gruesome picture of the degradation of the life of the flesh and the need to renounce it while there is yet time. Balahvar (Barlaam) and his preaching were a determining factor in the conversion of the great Russian novelist Leo Tolstoy—a discovery which we owe to Mr Tom Foley of Los Angeles. According to Tolstoy's autobiographical tract, *A Confession*, the following fable made a particular impres' sion on his mind; it is the third parable in the Georgian version.

The Man and the Elephant

Balahvar said: This transitory life resembles a man pursued by a raging elephant. And it cornered him inside a fearsome abyss. Then he caught sight of some trees onto which he climbed, and then saw two mice, one black and one white, which were gnawing away the roots of the trees up which the man had clambered. And he looked down into the chasm and noticed a dragon, which had parted its jaws and was intent on swallowing him. And he looked up above and saw a little honey trickling down the trees, and he began to lick it up. And now he remembered no longer the peril into which he had fallen. But the mice gnawed through the trees, and the man fell down, and the elephant seized him and hurled him over to the dragon.

Now, O king's son, that elephant is the image of death, which pursues the sons of men; and the trees are this transi' tory existence; and the mice are days and nights; and the honey is the sweetness of the passing world; and the savour of the passing world diverts mankind. So the days and nights are accomplished and death seizes him and the dragon swallows him down into hell: and this is the life of men.

Also of particular interest is Balahvar's first parable, that of the Trumpet of Death and the Four Caskets, which was ultimately adapted by Shakespeare in *The Merchant of Venice*:

> All that glisters is not gold;
> Often have you heard that told:
> Many a man his life hath sold
> But my outside to behold:
> Gilded tombs do worms infold . . .

The Georgian version runs as follows:

Once upon a time there was a king who was virtuous and sought after righteousness. And when he was passing along the road one day with a throng of followers, he caught sight of certain men clothed in ragged and torn garments, with complexions of yellow hue. But the king recognized them, and he quickly got down from his horse and embraced their necks. When his noblemen saw this, they considered the king's conduct highly eccentric, but did not dare to interfere. Afterwards they went to see the king's brother, who used to speak his mind frankly to him; and they said to him: 'Tell your brother never to do such a thing again; for he has been making obeisance to some ragged men.' So that brother came and told the king his views on the affair; but he gave him no answer.

And it was the custom in that kingdom that when the king was angry with anyone, he sent his slaves and the trumpet of death was sounded before the man's gates. And after a few days he sent some slaves, and told them: 'Go and blow the trumpet of death at my brother's gates.' So they went and did so.

When the king's brother heard this sound, he was afraid and began to weep and repine. Afterwards he put on mourning garments and went out with his wife and children to the gates of the king his brother; and they sprinkled ashes upon their heads. Then he ordered them to be led into his presence. But they were weeping. Then the king said to his brother: 'How is it that you were afraid at your own brother's herald? Do you not know that your brother and the heralds are but mortal men, and unable either to hasten the fulfilment of His will, or to avert what is destined to come upon them? And how was it that you were astonished at my falling down before those who were the heralds of Our Lord Jesus Christ, who were reminding and warning me of eternal condemnation? Thereby I have been made aware of my many sins against Him. But I shall unmask the conduct of those people who complained to you about me, saying: "Why ever did he make obeisance to the servants of God?"'

At the next opportunity, the king entered his treasury and fetched caskets adorned with gold and jewels. And he also had a load of stinking refuse brought, and dead men's bones and other loathsome trash. And he stuffed all this inside the caskets and fastened them on top with his seal. Then again he fetched other caskets, of plain manufacture, smeared with tar; and he placed within these some precious gems and whatever he could find that was best in his treasury, in addition to many perfumes. And these he sealed up also. Then he summoned his noblemen together, and when there was merrymaking, he ordered his treasurer to bring the caskets. And when he had laid them out, he told his nobles to appraise the caskets. But they failed to fathom the matter, and said to the king: 'Those plain caskets are unfit to be brought inside your palace; but the gilt ones are valuable beyond price.'

Then he ordered those caskets whose value they estimated highly to be opened. They threw them open, and there arose a nauseous stink, from which they shielded their faces with their sleeves. And they tipped out all manner of loathsome stuff. But then he ordered the mean-looking caskets to be opened; and there arose from them the scent of perfume which concealed all the disgusting smell. And out of these they tipped adornments of great price and precious jewels.

And the king said: 'Understand this, all you noblemen! It is we who are the caskets made beautiful without, we who deck out our exterior with multi-coloured apparel, whereas our soul within is full of sin and filth. But those who humble themselves for the sake of God and His name, and embrace poverty with fasting and prayer, and become yellow of complexion—the soul of these within is full of fragrance like the perfume stored within those caskets; and they shine before God just as do those precious gems. Now do you blame me for greeting those men of God, whose inward being is like to this?'

In the sequel to the story, Iodasaph is converted to Christianity and baptized by Balahvar (Barlaam). King Abenes his father is furious at the news, and redoubles his persecution of the Christian believers. However, Iodasaph triumphantly overcomes all further trials and temptations. Eventually King Abenes resolves to divide up his realm between himself and his son. The young prince's domains prosper, while his father's decline. The king is ultimately convinced of the truth of the Christian faith, and is converted along with all his followers. After the death of Abenes, Iodasaph hands the whole kingdom over to another Christian, Barakhia (here we have an echo of the Buddha's Great Renunciation), and departs to Ceylon. There he is reunited with Balahvar, and they both die in the odour of sanctity.

Among the many ramifications of this Bodhisattva legend, special interest attaches to its use by the founder and adepts of the Ahmadi movement in Islam, which has many adherents in India and the West. According to Ahmadi tradition, there lived in Kashmir some nineteen centuries ago a saint named Yuz Asaf, who preached in parables and used many of the same themes as did Christ Himself, as, for instance, that of the Sower from the New Testament. Yuz Asaf's shrine is at Srinagar in Kashmir, and the Ahmadi theory is that Yuz Asaf and Jesus are one and the same person, and that Jesus Christ after the Resurrection continued His missionary journeys as far as India and finally died there. This legend of Christ's tomb at Srinagar, fanciful though it is, is examined by Mr Robert Graves and Mr Joshua Podro in their monograph, *Jesus in Rome: A Historical Conjecture* (1957). However, even a superficial reading of the sources quoted suffices to show that they have no possible bearing on the life of Christ, but are simply a reflection of the story of Gautama Buddha and his missionary journeys, as transmitted in the Arabic version of the Barlaam and Josaphat legend, known as the *Book of Bilawhar and Budhasaf*; this Arabic text itself contains the Parable of the Sower introduced from the New Testament. Even the name of the town where Yuz Asaf is said to be buried, Srinagar, apparently arises from confusion with Kusinagara, where the Buddha ended his life on earth.

Far to the West, the story of Barlaam and Josaphat exerted a strong influence on the medieval Albigensian heretics of Provence, and is sometimes taken to be a Cathar religious tract. Barlaam and Josaphat were officially venerated as saints of the principal Catholic and Orthodox Churches. All these developments stem from this ancient Buddhist legend, to which the Georgians first gave a specific Christian colouring.

These Georgian Athonites, who founded the Iviron monastery on Mount Athos about the year 980, made a remarkable contribution to Georgian literature and culture. Euthymius and his successor Giorgi the Hagiorite (1009–65) revised virtually the whole corpus of Georgian ecclesiastical literature by reference to Greek manuscripts available to them through the great libraries of Constantinople. Euthymius rendered into Georgian many important books overlooked by previous translators, including the Revelation of St John the Divine, and codified Georgian Church law according to the Byzantine canons. Giorgi the Hagiorite tells us that much of this work was done at night by candlelight, after a full day spent in administering the Lavra and in religious exercises. 'The blessed Euthymius went on translating without respite and gave himself no repose; day and night he distilled the sweet honey of the books of God, with which he adorned our language and our Church. He translated so many divine works that nobody could enumerate them, since he worked at his translations not only on Mount Olympus and Mount Athos (which works we can list in detail), but also in Constantinople, and while travelling, and in all kinds of other places.' The unshakably orthodox doc-trines of the Georgian Athonites are well expressed in a spirited dialogue between Giorgi the Hagiorite and Patriarch Theo-dosius III of Antioch, in which Giorgi declared: 'Most Reverend Lord, your words are: "I sit upon the throne of Peter, chief of the Apostles." But we Georgians are the heirs and the flock of him who was first called—that is, St Andrew—and who called his brother; by him we too were converted and enlightened. What is more, one of the Twelve Holy Apostles, namely Simon the Canaanite, is buried in our land, in Abkha-zia, at the place which is called Nicopsia. Through these Holy Apostles we received the light; and since we came to know the One God, we have never renounced Him, nor has our nation ever turned aside into heretical ways, but we curse and anathe-matize all apostates and renegades. We stand firmly based on this rock of orthodoxy, and on the precepts which were pro-claimed by these Holy Apostles.' The story of St Andrew's mission to Georgia is now thought to be mythical, but no more so than many other respectable traditions current in medieval Christendom.

The work of the Georgian Athonites was worthily continued by Ephrem Mtsire (1027–94), translator of the works of St John Damascene, Ephraim the Syrian, St John Chrysostom and Dionysius the Areopagite, and author of an original bio/graphy of Simeon Metaphrastes, as well as being a leader of the Georgian monastic community on the Black Mountain close to Antioch; also by Arsen of Iqalto (d. 1125), the learned Rector of Iqalto academy near Telavi in Kakheti. Excellent work was also done at the Monastery of the Cross near Jeru/salem, built on the site of another ancient foundation by St Prochorus the Georgian, a disciple of Euthymius, about the year 1030. This monastery became the centre of Georgian cul/ture in the Holy Land, and the remains of its valuable library, including some 160 manuscripts, are now preserved in the Greek Patriarchate. The Monastery of the Cross is associated with Georgia's national poet, Shota Rustaveli, who is said to have retired to Jerusalem as a monk, and died and been buried there. A coloured fresco, freshly uncovered in the monastery buildings, shows Rustaveli in rich court dress, no doubt during a pilgrimage in the course of his earlier secular life.

Plate 71

Towards the end of the eleventh century, the Church's monopoly in literature and learning was being challenged from various quarters and subjected to severe strain. With the emer/gence of Georgia into the international arena, and increasing contacts with the brilliant civilization of contemporary Islam, Georgian philosophers and poets became impatient at the rigid trammels imposed by the churchmen. The Georgian kings, like contemporary Persian and Turkish sultans, were great patrons of the Arts, and favoured court poets and story/tellers equally with monastic chroniclers and other holy men. Ioane Shavteli wrote a verse panegyric of King David the Builder under the title *Abdul-Mesia* or 'Slave of the Messiah', while Chakhrukhadze composed a magnificent ode to Queen Tamar and her consort, David Soslan. The picaresque cycle of tales of adventure known as *Amiran-Darejaniani* was put together in prose form by Moses of Khoni, while Sargis of Tmogvi adapted the passionate and deeply felt story of the loves of Vis and Ramin from the Persian version by Fakhr al-Din Gurgani, itself an elaboration of an old Parthian romance. Vis and Ramin are slaves of relentless fate at its most inexorable —'Vénus toute entière à sa proie attachée'—and their long-thwarted, often despairing passion may be compared with that of Tristan and Isolde. In the case of Vis and Ramin, however, torment is followed by married bliss, in which the lovers are portrayed as passing no less than eighty-one years together! To give some idea of the emotional force of this classic work, we cite Ramin's lament over the body of the departed Vis, in the fine translation by Sir Oliver Wardrop:

O beloved friend, more to be desired than life! Thou art gone, thou hast forsaken me completely, and hast left me heart-branded, consumed, weary of the world. . . . None ever had a friend like thee! Now, why art thou become weary of me? Hast thou not oft sworn fidelity to me? Now, because of what sin art thou become merciless? Why hast thou broken thine oath to me? For so long we have been united in soul, affectionate, why hast thou made me to lament? But as I know thy heart, certainly thou didst not deceive me. It is evidently Fate that has betrayed me, and from it this is no marvel. To whom has it fulfilled good from then till now? The earth is emptied of joy by thy departure, thou hast taken every-thing good with thee. How can I endure the plague of old age and feebleness, as well as the sadness of being bereft of thee? Or how can I live and endure the thought of this? Grief is added to grief! I lying on a throne, and thou in the earth—I cannot think of it!

This efflorescence of secular love poetry, romance and epic was not confined to court circles. As early as the twelfth century, the Georgians of all social classes had acquired a rich store of folk tales, popular epics and drinking songs, many of them having their roots in remote antiquity. Contact with medieval Byzantium and Iran, and increased opportunities for travel and trade throughout the East, enriched this store of material still further. In many instances, motifs of foreign provenance were greatly modified in their new Caucasian setting, and transformed into fresh and spontaneous imaginative creations of the folk mind. This was the case, for instance, with the *Shahnameh* or *Book of Kings* of Firdawsi (940–1020), which early became popular in Georgia under the title *Rostomiani*, after Rustam, one of the legendary heroes commemorated in the great Persian epic. Many versions, in verse and prose, circulated in Georgia from an early date. The *Amiran-Darejaniani* of Moses of Khoni, a work put into literary shape on Georgian soil, also gave rise to a whole cycle of legends, elaborated and handed down by the village story-teller. So involved has the interrelation of the literary and folk variants become that some leading experts, such as Professor Mikheil Chikovani of Tbilisi University, would even argue that the folk variants preceded the literary *Amiran-Darejaniani*, rather than being derived from it.

Fig. 47. Georgian medieval helmet styles. Detail from MS. H 1665, Institute of Manuscripts, Tbilisi. Fifteenth century

A beautiful and indisputably original Georgian popular romance is that of Abesalom and Eteri, known as *Eteriani*, which has been made into a magnificent opera by the Georgian composer Zakaria Paliashvili. Eteri is a Georgian Cinderella, hounded and starved by a wicked stepmother. One day, a kindly witch clothes her in silk and sends her to church, where she attracts the attention of the prince, Abesalom. Returning home, Eteri drops one of her shoes in a stream. Abesalom finds the shoe and ultimately succeeds in tracing her. The lovers' happiness is destroyed by Abesalom's trusted retainer, an Iago-like character called Murman. The devil shows Murman how to win Eteri for himself, namely by sprinkling her with millet, which turns into loathsome fleas and lice, which only Murman's touch can momentarily cleanse. Filled with bitterness, Abesalom abandons Eteri to Murman's embraces.

Abesalom pines away, and soon lies at death's door. As a last resort, he sends Murman away in search of the waters of immortality. Murman spends one last night with Eteri, greeting the morn of his departure with these lines:

> O night now upon us,
> Turn not too soon to dawn;
> Else my love will fly away
> And tomorrow I shall see her no more.

While Murman is away, Abesalom breathes his last. Eteri stabs herself. The unhappy lovers are buried together. At the head of their tomb, a vine springs up, at their feet a spring of fresh water. From Abesalom's body, there grows a rose, from Eteri's a violet. Murman returns from his quest, digs himself a grave between the two lovers, and kills himself upon the spot. Thenceforward the spring of water is poisoned, the vine languishes, and a hideous thorn bush grows up from Murman's corpse. When the violet and the rose seek to entwine and cling together, the thorn bush puts out a branch and forces them apart once more.

Profane love poetry could, if necessary, be justified as a harmless diversion for kings and princes. Innovations in religious dogma were, from the viewpoint of strict orthodoxy, far more dangerous. In this respect, the philosophical work of the great Georgian neo-Platonist Ioane Tchimtchimeli, known as Petritsi (d. 1125), posed a serious challenge. Petritsi's life-work was directed towards founding a national Georgian school of metaphysical philosophy, reconciling reason with revelation, and harmonizing Christian dogma with the teach-ing of the Greek philosophers, notably Plato. Ioane Tchim-tchimeli was educated at the Mangana Academy in Con-stantinople, his teachers being the famous Johannes Italos and

Michael Psellos (1018–79), who revived the cult of Plato and the Ancients, and laid the foundations of medieval humanism. A Greek source speaks of a certain 'Abasgian', *i.e.* Georgian, as one of Johannes Italos' most faithful disciples, and no doubt this refers to Ioane Tchimtchimeli. Around 1076, he returned to his Georgian homeland, but like his own teachers in Byzantium, found his ideas uncongenial and himself unwelcome among the conservative Church hierarchy. In 1083 he accepted an invitation from the Byzantine soldier and statesman Grigol Bakurianisdze—himself of Caucasian origin—to study and lecture at the newly founded seminary of Petritsoni at Bachkovo in Bulgaria, to which Ioane owes his surname of Petritsi. Eventually Petritsi was reconciled with the Georgian Church authorities and returned to his native land under the patronage of King David the Builder, to play a prominent part in organizing the Georgian academy at Gelati.

Plate 52

Petritsi was the first Georgian theologian to go back direct to the Greek classical thinkers Plato and Aristotle; he translated into Georgian two treatises of Aristotle (these renderings are lost), as well as two neoPlatonist works, *On Human Nature* by Nemesius of Emesa(*fl.* 390)—an attempt to compile a system of anthropology from the standpoint of Christian philosophy allied to Platonic doctrines of preexistence and metempsychosis —and the *Elements of Theology* by Proclus Diadochus (410– 485), to which Petritsi added his own extensive commentary. Petritsi's translation, based on ancient manuscripts, has been used with profit by Proclus' English editor, Professor E. R. Dodds, while his commentary convinces one of the onset of philosophical maturity in Georgia, and the possibility of independent achievement in the realm of metaphysics. Petritsi was a valiant and original spirit, perhaps the most talented philosopher Georgia has produced. He attempted, so he avowed, to summon Athena, Hermes and Prometheus to his aid in interpreting the divine message of the Supreme Logos, Jesus Christ,

Fig. 48. Lady with unicorn. Georgian costume detail from MS. H 1665, Institute of Manuscripts, Tbilisi. Fifteenth century

and to ally the Christian faith to the highest forms of antique philosophy. But herein he was trying to reconcile the irreconcil‑able, and it was inevitable that his writings should arouse oppo‑sition among the conventional scholastics of his time. Only in the eighteenth century could the learned Catholicos Patriarch Antoni I declare Petritsi to be his favourite theologian, 'a godly philosopher, the sun of our nation'—a verdict fully supported by modern scholarship.

Plate 72

The summit of this efflorescence of Georgian literature and philosophy in the Middle Ages is reached in the epic by Shota Rustaveli, *Vepkhistqaosani*, 'The Knight in the Panther's Skin', in which the currents of Platonist philosophy and Eastern romance find their harmonious and inspired fusion. Of the poet's life we know little for certain—scarcely more than he himself gives in the prologue and epilogue of his poem, which are in fact thought to have been added by a later hand. 'By shedding tears of blood', the bard exclaims, 'we extol the sovereign Tamar, whose praises I, not ill-chosen, have told forth . . . They bade me indite sweet verses in her praise, laud her eyebrows and lashes, her hair, her lips and teeth, cut crystal and ruby arrayed in ranks. An anvil of soft lead breaks even hard stone.' In the epilogue, the poet (or his imitator) explains that he is a certain Meskhian, a native of the little town of Rustavi, hence the surname Rustaveli. Legend adds further that the bard was educated at Athens, had travelled much in Asia, and then held the post of treasurer to Queen Tamar, with whom he fell madly in love. 'For her whom a multitude of hosts obey, I lose my wits, I die! I am sick of love, and for me there is no cure from anywhere, unless she give me healing or the earth a grave.' It was the queen's disdain that led Rustaveli to withdraw from secular life and finish his days at the Monastery of the Cross at Jerusalem, where his picture appears on a fresco. Most of this, admittedly, is legend, and as is the case with the 'Baconian' school of Shakespeare criticism, there are some who dismiss as untrue the entire tradition relating to Rustaveli's date and personality. The late Dr Jaromír Jedlička, for instance, an outstanding scholar who translated Rustaveli into Czech, declared in a private letter dated May 31 1959 his belief that 'the *Vepkhistqaosani* was not written in the time of Tamar, its author is not Rustaveli, and the Prologue and Epilogue were written much later than the poem itself.'

Fig. 48

Plate 71

However this may be, there is no denying the universal inspiration and appeal of Rustaveli's poem, which has been translated several times into Russian (once by Constantine Bal'mont), three times into French, and also into English, German, Spanish, Italian, Hungarian, Czech, Armenian and Japanese. Seldom has a poet's vision been so vast, comprehensive and turbulent, so that it seems that the universe is about to clash in primeval chaos, until the creative breath of a great poet subdues this chaos to a severe harmony. The sublime tone

of the work is set from the opening lines, where the bard in-
vokes the single, supreme Deity.—'He who created the firma-
ment, by that mighty power made beings inspired from on high
with souls celestial; to us men He has given the world, infinite
in variety we possess it; from Him is every monarch in His
likeness.' It is noticeable that Rustaveli's God is a universal
force, and that there is never any mention of individual members of the Holy Trinity, or any of the conventional Christian
religious symbolism. After discussing the merits of various
forms of minstrelsy, and defining the differences separating ideal
from profane love, Rustaveli exclaims: 'I speak of the highest
love—divine in its kind. It is difficult to discourse thereon, ill
to tell forth with tongues. It is heavenly, upraising the soul on
pinions.' It is, in short, no common mortal love of which
Rustaveli sings, but the single-minded, idealized cult of which
the Platonists discoursed, in whose name knights of old did
battle for their beloved, and of which troubadours and other
exponents of courtly love sing in sweet despair.

While his poem is an allegory on Georgia's heroic age,
Rustaveli chose an exotic setting for its narrative framework,
which he claims to have found in some old Persian tale. The
venerable King Rostevan of Arabia gives up his throne to his
daughter Tinatin—as in fact King Giorgi III of Georgia did
in favour of Queen Tamar, his own daughter. A great feast
is arranged at court, then a hunt during which the king and
his suite encounter a knight clad in a panther's skin sitting by
a river, sobbing bitterly. Rostevan gets no reply to his greeting,
and orders the stranger to be seized and brought to him by force;
but the knight jumps on to his steed, kills his assailants, and
vanishes amid general consternation. Queen Tinatin is deeply
intrigued by this mysterious episode. She summons her beloved,
Avtandil, commander of the royal army, and begs him to set
out in quest of the stranger, promising him her hand when he
returns.

Plate 74k

After long and tiresome travels, Avtandil runs to earth the man of mystery in a desert cave. The meeting of the two heroes is very touching and they soon become intimate. The man in the panther's skin is named Tariel, and tells Avtandil his tragic life story. He is a prince and general of India, the affianced of Nestan-Darejan, daughter of the Indian emperor. At Nestan's instigation, Tariel murdered her first betrothed, a Persian prince, to save her from a hateful match and guarantee the succession to the Indian throne from foreign usurpers. Hereupon riots broke out in the kingdom, and Nestan was secretly abducted from the palace. Since then Tariel has abandoned the world of men and roamed through the deserts of the world, looking for his beloved and bewailing his sad fate.

Avtandil comforts Tariel, and swears to remain for ever his faithful friend—indeed, the ideal of loyalty and friendship is one of the *leitmotifs* of Rustaveli's poem. Avtandil returns to Arabia to report to Tinatin on his discovery, and then the two friends set off again to scour the world for Nestan-Darejan. After many vicissitudes, and thanks to an adventure as amorous as it is comic, Avtandil comes at last upon the princess' trail, shut up in a remote fortress in the land of the *Kajis* or demons, to whose prince she is to be forcibly wed. With the help of a third hero, Pridon, the two knights raise an army, besiege the castle and rescue the princess. Then follows feasting and merry-making, first at Pridon's palace, then in Arabia at King Rostevan's court, afterwards in India. Tariel and Nestan-Darejan ascend the throne of their ancestors in India, and Avtandil and Tinatin rule in felicity over the Arabian kingdom.

The poet's range of interest is amazingly wide; it embraces a mastery of political and judicial questions, familiarity with court life and ceremonial, and a grasp of the subtleties of the art of war. He can portray the manifold aspects of a great sea-power, its crowded cities and ports teeming with life and activity, and the feverish speculations and shifting fortunes of its

inhabitants. Rustaveli was familiar with ancient Greek philosophy, with astronomy and astrology, and with the poetry of his
Persian contemporary, Nizami of Ganja (1140–1202).

Whether Rustaveli is writing of the laws of the feudal system;
the code of knightly love, fealty and honour; the dealings of
merchants, their avarice and thirst for gain; or the subtle inner
conflicts of the human soul, he brings the same zest to his pen,
using the same colourful imagery and broad human sympathy.
Even today there exist many Georgian peasants who know by
heart whole cantos of the epic, and recite them just as the
Persian countryman will recite the verse of Hafiz or Sa'di. A
copy of *Vepkhistqaosani* traditionally forms part of the dowry of
every self-respecting Georgian bride. Whether approved by the
Orthodox Church or no, Rustaveli's ethical code, with its
emphasis on courage, loyalty and patriotism, is well attuned to
the Georgian national character.

Like certain other great poets, Rustaveli does not shrink on
occasion from grotesque humour, even from bathos, which
may even be said to heighten the general effect of his masterpiece. At one point for instance, Avtandil finds himself obliged
to make love to a mature lady named Dame Fatman, his hos-
tess at the city of Gulansharo. Thinking of his absent love, the
fair Tinatin, Avtandil muses: 'Behold me, O lovers, me who
have a rose of mine own! Away from her, I the nightingale, like
a carrion crow, sit on the dung-heap.' Swooning with desire,
Dame Fatman feels no such repugnance. Rustaveli comments
sardonically: 'If a crow finds a rose, it deems even itself to be a
nightingale.'

Rustaveli is a master of the technical art of versification. He
wrote in stanzas composed of four lines or *shairi* of sixteen
syllables, the rhyme scheme being *a:a:a:a*. Such a metre makes
great demands on the poet, especially as each rhyme is usually
made up of two or even three matching final syllables, and not
the last syllable alone, as often occurs in English verse.

Fig. 49. Georgian noble ladies' costume, twelfth–
thirteenth centuries

As a result of the Mongol, Persian and Turkish invasions, and the disapproval of the Church, the oldest manuscripts of the poem were destroyed. The most ancient complete copies, several finely illustrated in the Persian manner, date from the seventeenth century. Recent researches by the staff of the Insti⁄tute of Manuscripts in Tbilisi have brought to light fragments of the poem from the sixteenth century, bound into covers of volumes in a provincial library in Akhaltsikhe. In the cave monastery of Vani, in Samtskhe province, destroyed by the Persians in 1552, there have been discovered a number of fifteenth⁄century *graffiti* on the walls, including stanzas 1300–1301 of Rustaveli's poem. Further finds will certainly enable us one day to reconstruct with greater certainty the authentic text of *Vepkhistqaosani*, and tell us more of the identity of its author and his life and times.

Plate 72

Their tale is ended like a dream of the night. They are passed away, gone beyond the world. Behold the treachery of time: to him who thinks it long, even for him it is of a moment ... This is such a world as is not be to trusted by any; it is a moment to the eyes of men, and only long enough for the blinking of the eyelashes. What is the use of searching and striving? Fate will put us to shame. Happy at least is he whom destiny escorts beyond this life into the hereafter!

Rustaveli's great poem is the swan song of Georgia's Golden Age. Between 1225 and 1240, Georgia was overwhelmed and devastated by Khwarazmian and Mongol hordes from central Asia, and again late in the fourteenth century by Leng Timur, or Tamburlane the Great. The feudal nobles exploited the situation by throwing off their allegiance to the monarchy, and setting up as petty sovereigns on their own. In 1453, Constantinople, centre of Eastern Christendom, fell to the Ottoman Turks. Georgia was partitioned between the Turkish Sultan and the Persian Shah. In spite of heroic efforts by King Erekle II in the eighteenth century, annexation by Russia proved the only solution to Georgia's problems. Today, Georgia is one of the most flourishing constituent republics of the Soviet Union. Her language, literature and history are taught in schools and institutions of higher learning, including Tbilisi State University and the Georgian Academy of Sciences, and her age-old culture lives again in the twentieth century. Active, if belated measures are being taken to protect for posterity some at least of the architectural monuments and artistic treasures of Georgia's antique and truly original civilization.

Bibliography

General Works and Background Reading

ALLEN, W. E. D. *A History of the Georgian People*. London, 1932.

APAKIDZE, A. M. and others. *Sakartvelos arkeologia* (Archaeology of Georgia). Tbilisi, 1959.

BADDELEY, J. F. *The Rugged Flanks of Caucasus*. 2 vols. Oxford, 1940.

BYHAN, A. *La Civilisation caucasienne*. Paris, 1936.

CHANTRE, E. *Recherches anthropologiques dans le Caucase*. 5 vols. Paris, Lyon, 1885–87.

GARDANOV, B. A. and others. *Narody Kavkaza* (Peoples of the Caucasus). vol. 2. (Series: *Narody Mira: Etnograficheskie ocherki*, ed. S. P. Tolstov.) Moscow, 1962.

GEIGER, B. and others. *Peoples and Languages of the Caucasus*. (*Janua Linguarum*, no. 6.) The Hague, 1959.

HANČAR, F. *Urgeschichte Kaukasiens*, Vienna, Leipzig, 1937.

JANASHIA, S. N. *Shromebi* (Historical studies) 3 vols. Tbilisi, 1949–59.

JAVAKHISHVILI, I. A. *Kartveli eris istoria* (History of the Georgian people), new ed., I, Tbilisi, 1960.

LANG, D. M. *A Modern History of Georgia*. London, 1962.

MELIKISHVILI, G. A. *K istorii drevnei Gruzii* (On the history of ancient Georgia). Tbilisi, 1959.

MONGAIT, A. *Archaeology in the U.S.S.R.* English trans. by D. Skvirsky. Moscow, 1959.

SALIA, K. ed., *Bedi Kartlisa, Le Destin de la Géorgie, Recueil historique, scientifique et littéraire géorgien*. Paris, 1948– . (In progress.)

SANDERS, A. (*pseud.* for Alexander Nikuradze). *Kaukasien, geschichtlicher Umriss*. Munich, 1942.

TBILISI, Academy of Sciences of the Georgian S.S.R., Institute of History named after Iv. Javakhishvili. *Masalebi Sakartvelos da Kavkasiis arkeologiisatvis*. (Materials for the Archaeology of Georgia and Caucasia.) 4 vols. Tbilisi, 1955–. (In progress.)

— State Museum of Georgia named after S. N. Janashia. *Bulletin du Musée de Géorgie*. vol. 1, etc., Tbilisi, 1920–. (In progress.)

TOKAREV, S. A. *Etnografiya narodov SSSR* (Ethnography of the peoples of the USSR). Moscow, 1958.

UVAROVA, COUNTESS P. S. ed. *Materialy po arkheologii Kavkaza.* (Materials for the Archaeology of the Caucasus). 13 vols. Moscow, 1888 *et seq.*

CHAPTER I

BERDZENISHVILI, N. Z. Khramis kheobis paleolituri dzeglebi (Paleo‑ lithic monument of the Khrami valley), in *Masalebi Sakartvelos da Kavkasiis arkeologiisatvis*, III, Tbilisi, 1963, pp. 5–16.

— *Kvis khanis akhali dzegli Dsqaldsitelis kheobashi* (A new Stone Age monument in the Dsqaldsitela valley). Tbilisi, 1964.

DEBETS, G. F. *Paleoantropologiya SSSR* (Palaeoanthropology of the U.S.S.R.), Moscow, 1948.

GRIGOLIA, G. K. *Paleolit Kvemo Kartli* (Palaeolithic cultures of Lower Kartli). Tbilisi, 1963.

KALANDADZE, A. N. Ostatki mezoliticheskoi i neoliticheskoi kul'tur v Gruzii (Remains of mesolithic and neolithic cultures in Georgia), in *Izvestiya Instituta Yazyka i Material'noi Kul'tury im. N. Ya. Marra* (Bulletin of the Marr Institute of Language and Material Culture), IV. Tbilisi, 1939.

KERND'L, A. Ubersicht über den Forschungsstand der Ur‑ und Früh‑ geschichte in der Sowjetunion, in *Berliner Jahrbuch für Vor‑ und Früh‑ geschichte*, I, III. Berlin, 1961, 1963.

KILADZE, N. Z. Neoliticheskie pamyatniki iz Tetramitsa (Neolithic monuments from Tetramidsa), in *Materialy po Istorii Gruzii i Kavkaza* (Materials for the History of Georgia and the Caucasus), pt. 29. Tbilisi, 1951.

KOROBKOV, I. I. Novye paleoliticheskie nakhodki na Yashtukhe (New Paleolithic finds from Yashtukha), in *Sovetskaya Arkheologiya*, 1965, fasc. 3.

LYUBIN, V. P. Vysokogornaya pechchernaya stoyanka Kudaro I (The mountain cave settlement of Kudaro I), in *Izvestiya Vsesoyuznogo Geograficheskogo Obshchestva* (Bulletin of the all‑Union Geographical Society), pt. 91. Moscow, 1959.

NIORADZE, G. K. *Paleolitichesky chelovek v peshchere Deviskhvreli* (Paleo‑ lithic man in the cavern of Devishkvreli) (Trudy Muzeya Gruzii. Works of the Georgian Museum. No. 6), Tbilisi, 1933.

ZAMYATNIN, S. N. *Ocherki po Paleolitu* (Paleolithic Studies). Moscow, Leningrad, 1961.

— *Paleolit Abkhazii* (The Paleolithic culture of Abkhazia). Sukhumi, 1937.

— Peshchernye navesy Mgvimevi bliz Chiatury, Gruziya (Cave shelters of Mghvimevi, near Chiatura, Georgia), in *Sovetskaya Arkheo‑ logiya*, III, 1937, pp. 57–75.

CHAPTER II

ABESADZE. Ts. N. and others. *K istorii medno‑bronzovoi metallurgii v Gruzii* (On the history of copper and bronze metallurgy in Georgia). Tbilisi, 1958.

ALBRIGHT, W. F. Ninib‑Ninurta, in *Journal of the American Oriental Society*, vol. 38, no. 3, 1918, pp. 197–201.

BURNEY, C. A. Eastern Anatolia in the Chalcolithic and Early Bronze Age, in *Anatolian Studies*, VIII, 1958, pp. 157–209.

CHUBINISHVILI, T. N. *Amiranis Gora. Materials on the ancient history of Meskhet‑Javakheti*. Tbilisi, 1963.

FORBES, R. J. *Metallurgy in Antiquity,* Leiden, 1950; new ed., in 2 vols. Leiden, 1964.

FRANKFORT, H. Sumerians, Semites and the Origin of Copper‑Working, in *Antiquaries Journal*, VIII, 1928, pp. 217–35.

GIMBUTAS, M. The Indo‑Europeans: Archaeological Problems, in *American Anthropologist*, vol. 65, no. 4, Aug. 1963, pp. 815–36.

GOETZE, A. *Kleinasien* (*Handbuch der Altertumswissenschaft—Kultur‑ geschichte des alten Orients*, Abschnitt 3, Lief. 1). Munich, 1957.

GURNEY, O. R. *The Hittites*. Rev. ed., London, 1964.

IESSEN, A. A. *K voprosu o drevneishei metallurgii medi na Kavkaze* (On the question of the most ancient copper metallurgy in the Caucasus). Moscow, Leningrad, 1935.

IVASHCHENKO, M. M. Beiträge zur Vorgeschichte Abchaziens, in *Eurasia Septentrionalis Antiqua*, VII, 1932, pp. 98–112.

JAPARIDZE, O. *Kartuli tomebis istoriisatvis litonis dsarmoebis adreul sapekhurze* (On the history of the Georgian tribes in the Early Bronze Age). Tbilisi, 1961.

JAVAKHISHVILI, A. I., and GLONTI, L. I. *Urbnisi* (Report of the Urbnisi archaeological expedition, 1954–61), vol. I. Tbilisi, 1962.

KORIDZE, D. L. *Materialuri kulturis udzvelesi dzeglebi* (Bronze Age finds from Sachkhere). Tbilisi, 1961.

KUFTIN, B. A. *Arkheologicheskaya marshrutnaya ekspeditsiya 1945 goda v Yugo-Osetiyu i Imeretiyu* (Archaeological explorations of 1945 in South Ossetia and Imereti). Tbilisi, 1949.

— *Arkheologicheskie raskopki v Trialeti* (Archaeological excavations in Trialeti). Vol. I, Tbilisi, 1941.

— *Arkheologicheskie raskopki 1947 goda v Tsalkinskom raione* (Archaeological excavations in 1947 in the Tsalka district). Tbilisi, 1948.

KUSHNAREVA, K. Kh., and CHUBINISHVILI, T. N. The Historical Significance of the Southern Caucasus in the Third Millennium BC, in *Soviet Anthropology and Archaeology*, II, no. 3, Winter 1963–64, pp. 3–16. (Trans. from *Sovetskaya Arkheologiya*, 1963, no. 3, pp. 10–24.)

MARR, N. Y., and SMIRNOV, Ya. I. *Les Vichaps.* Leningrad, 1931.

MELIKISHVILI, G. A. Vozniknovenie Khettskogo tsarstva i problema drevneishego naseleniya Zakavkaz'ya i Maloy Azii (The Origins of the Hittite kingdom and the problem of the most ancient population of Transcaucasia and Asia Minor), in *VDI*, 1965, I, pp. 3–30.

MELLAART, J. The end of the Early Bronze Age in Anatolia and the Aegean, in *American Journal of Archaeology*, vol. 62, no. 1, Jan. 1958, pp. 9–33.

PKHAKADZE, G. G. *Eneolit Kvemo Kartli: Eneoliticheskie pamyatniki Kiketi* (The Eneolithic culture of Lower Kartli: Eneolithic remains from Kiketi). Tbilisi, 1963.

SCHAEFFER, C. F. A. Archaeological discoveries in Trialeti—Caucasus, in *Journal of the Royal Asiatic Society*, April, 1944.

TALLGREN, A. M. Sur les monuments mégalithiques du Caucase occidental, in *Eurasia Septentrionalis Antiqua*, IX, 1934, pp. 1–46.

TAVADZE, P. and SAQVARELIDZE, T. *Bronzy drevnei Gruzii* (Bronzes of ancient Georgia, with English summary). Tbilisi, 1959.

TSERETELI, M. The Asianic (Asia Minor) elements in national Georgian paganism, in *Georgica*, I, pt. 1, London, 1935.

ZAKHAROV, A. A. Études sur l'archéologie de l'Asie Mineure et du Caucase, in *Revue hittite et asianique*, vol. 4. Paris, 1931.

CHAPTER III

APOLLONIUS RHODIUS. *Argonautica. Or, the Quest of Jason for the Golden Fleece . . . together with the translation into English prose by Edward P. Coleridge; with a preface by Moses Hadas, and illustrations by A. Tassos.* New York, 1960.

CARTER, D. *The Symbol of the Beast: The Animal-Style Art of Eurasia.* New York, 1957.

CAVAIGNAC, E. Mushki et Phrygiens, in *Journal Asiatique*, vol. 241, 1953, pp. 139–43.

DE MORGAN, J. *Mission scientifique au Caucase.* 2 vols. Paris, 1889.

DE PLANHOL, X. 'Geographica Pontica, I–II', in *Journal Asiatique*, 1963, pts. 3–4, pp. 293–309.

DIRR, A. *Caucasian Folk-tales.* London, 1925.

HERODOTUS. *The Histories.*

HILLS, D. C. *My Travels in Turkey.* London, 1964.

LANG, D. M. and MEREDITH-OWENS, G. M. *Amiran-Darejaniani*, in *Bulletin of the School of African and Oriental Studies*, XXII, pt. 3, 1959, pp. 454–90.

MELIKISHVILI, G. A. *Nairi-Urartu.* Tbilisi, 1954.

— *Urartskie klinoobraznye nadpisi* (Urartian cuneiform inscriptions). Moscow, 1960.

MELIKSET-BEGI, L. M. *Megalituri kultura Sakartveloshi* (Megalithic culture in Georgia). Tbilisi, 1938.

MELLINK, M. J. Meshech, in *The Interpreter's Dictionary of the Bible*, III, pp. 357–8.

PITSKHELAURI, K. N. Brinjaos kakhuri tipis satevari (The Kakhetian type of Bronze Dagger), in *Masalebi Sakartvelos da Kavkasiis arkeologiisat-vis*, II, Tbilisi, 1959, pp. 109–37.

THOMSON, J. O. *History of Ancient Geography.* Cambridge, 1948.

TSITLANADZE, L. G. Qazbegis gandzis zogierti sakitkhisatvis (Problems relating to the Kazbek Hoard), in *Masalebi Sakartvelos da Kavkasiis arkeologiisatvis*, III, Tbilisi, 1963, pp. 39–59.

XENOPHON. *Anabasis*.

CHAPTER IV

APAKIDZE, A. M. *Goroda i gorodskaya zhizn' v drevnei Gruzii* (Towns and urban life in ancient Georgia), vol. I. Tbilisi, 1963.

—, and others. *Mtskheta. Itogi arkheologicheskikh issledovanii* (Mtskheta. Results of the field excavations), vol. I. Georgian edition, Tbilisi, 1955; Russian edition, 1958.

GDZELISHVILI, I. A. *Zheleznoplavil'noe proizvodstvo v drevnei Gruzii* (Iron production and smelting in ancient Georgia). Tbilisi, 1964.

GOBEJISHVILI, G. F. *Arkheologicheskie raskopki v Sovetskoi Gruzii* (Archaeological researches in Soviet Georgia). Tbilisi, 1952.

IVASHCHENKO, M. M. Kuvshinny mogil'nik v zapadnoi Gruzii (An urn-burial cemetery in Western Georgia), in *Sovetskaya Arkheologiya*, vol. 13, 1950.

KAPANADZE, D. G. *Gruzinskaya numizmatika* (Georgian numismatics). Moscow, 1955.

KLIMOV, G. A. *Etimologichesky slovar' kartvel'skikh yazykov* (Etymological dictionary of the Kartvelian languages). Moscow, 1964.

KUFTIN, B. A. *Materialy k arkheologii Kolkhidy* (Materials on the archaeology of Colchis). 2 vols. Tbilisi, 1949–50.

LANG, D. M. *Studies in the Numismatic History of Georgia in Transcaucasia* (Numismatic Notes and Monographs, no. 130). New York, 1955.

LATYSHEV, V. V. *Izvestiya drevnikh pisatelei o Skithii i Kavkaze: Scythica et Caucasica* (Reports of ancient writers on Scythia and the Caucasus). 2 vols. St Petersburg, 1890–1906.

— New edition, in *Vestnik Drevnei Istorii*, 1947, no. 1, et seq.

LOMTATIDZE, G. A. *Kldeetis samarovani* (The Kldeeti cemetery of the second century AD). Tbilisi, 1957.

SIKHARULIDZE, I. M. *Atcharis materialuri kulturis dzeglebi* (Monuments of the material culture of Atchara). Batumi, 1962.

SMIRNOV, Ya. I. *Akhalgoriisky klad* (The Akhalgori hoard). Tbilisi, 1934. (Also a German edition: *Der Schatz von Achalgori*.)

TSERETELI, G. V. Armazskaya bilingva (The bilingual inscription from Armazi), in *Izvestiya Instituta Yazyka i Material'noi Kul'tury* (Bulletin of the Institute of Language and Material Culture), XIII. Tbilisi, 1942.

CHAPTER V

BERDZENISHVILI, N. A., and others. *Istoriya Gruzii* (History of Georgia). Vol. 1. Tbilisi, 1962.

BROSSET, M.-F., and CHUBINOV, D. I., *ed.* and *trans.* *Histoire de la Géorgie depuis l'Antiquité jusqu'au XIXe siècle.* 7 vols. St Petersburg, 1849–58.

CONSTANTINE PORPHYROGENITUS, Byzantine emperor. *De Adminis-trando Imperio.* Vol. 1 (text), *ed.* Gy. Moravcsik, Budapest, 1949; vol. 2 (commentary), *ed.* R. J. H. Jenkins. London, 1962.

DER NERSESSIAN, S. *Armenia and the Byzantine Empire.* Harvard, 1947.

GREKOV, B. D., and others. *Ocherki istorii SSSR: Period Feodalizma, IX–XV v.v.* (Studies in the History of the U.S.S.R.: Period of Feudalism, ninth to fifteenth centuries.) 2 vols. Moscow, 1953.

GROUSSET, R. *Histoire de l'Arménie des origines à 1071.* Paris, 1947.

KARST, J., *ed.* *Corpus Juris Ibero-Caucasici.* (A collection of medieval Georgian law codes, with French trans. 6 vols.) Strasbourg, 1934–40.

LANG, D. M. *The Last Years of the Georgian Monarchy.* New York, 1957.

MINORSKY, V. *A History of Sharvan and Darband.* Cambridge, 1958.

— Article 'Tiflis' in *Encyclopaedia of Islam.*

MOVSES DASKHURANCI. *A History of the Caucasian Albanians,* trans. by C. J. F. Dowsett. Oxford, 1961.

SCHLUMBERGER, G. *L'Epopée Byzantine à la fin du dixième siècle.* New ed. Paris, 1925.

TOUMANOFF, C. *Studies in Christian Caucasian History.* Georgetown, 1963.

CHAPTER VI

ADAMIA, I. *Kartuli khalkhuri khurotmodzghvreba: Atchara* (Georgian popular architecture: Atchara province). Tbilisi, 1956.

ALADASHVILI, N. A. *Nikordsmindis reliepebi* (The bas-reliefs of Nikords-minda church). Tbilisi, 1957.

ALIBEGASHVILI, G. V. *Chetyre portreta tsaritsy Tamary* (Four portraits of Queen Tamar). Tbilisi, 1957.

AMIRANASHVILI, Sh. Ia. *Beka Opizari* (An account of the twelfth century Georgian goldsmith). Tbilisi, 1939.

— *Les Émaux de Géorgie* (Merveilles de l'Art en Orient). Paris, 1962.

— *Istoriya gruzinskogo iskusstva* (History of Georgian Art). Moscow, 1963.

— *Istoriya gruzinskoi monumental'noi zhivopisi* (History of Georgian mural painting), vol. 1. Tbilisi, 1957.

ARS GEORGICA. *Kartuli khelovneba.* (Works of the Institute of the History of Georgian Art.) Tbilisi, 1942–. In progress.

BABENCHIKOV, M. V. *Narodnoe dekorativnoe iskusstvo Zakavkaz'ya* (Popular decorative art of Transcaucasia). Moscow, 1948.

BALTRUŠAITIS, J. *Études sur l'art médiéval en Géorgie et en Arménie.* Paris, 1929.

BERIDZE, V. V. *Samtskhis khurotmodzghvreba* (The Architecture of Samtskhe, thirteenth to sixteenth centuries). Tbilisi, 1955.

—, and others. *Arkhitektura Respublik Zakavkaz'ya* (Architecture of the Transcaucasian Republics). Moscow, 1951.

BUXTON, D. R. *Russian Mediaeval Architecture.* Cambridge, 1934.

CHKHIKVADZE, G. Z., and others. *Gruzinskaya muzikal'naya kul'tura* (Georgian musical culture). Moscow, 1957.

CHOPIKASHVILI, N. V. *Kartuli kostiumi, VI–XIV ss.* (Georgian costume of the sixth to fourteenth centuries). Tbilisi, 1964.

CHUBINASHVILI, G. N. *Arkhitektura Kakhetii* (The Architecture of Kakheti). 2 vols. Tbilisi, 1956–59.

— *Kartuli okromtchedloba VIII–XVIII saukuneebisa* (Georgian gold repoussé work of the eighth to eighteenth centuries). Tbilisi, 1957.

— *Pamyatniki tipa Dzhvari* (Georgian church architecture of the type of Mtskheta Jvari). 2 vols. Tbilisi, 1948.

— *Peshchernye monastyri David-Garedzhi* (The cave monasteries of David-Garesja). Tbilisi, 1948.

CHUBINASHVILI, N. *Gruzinskaya srednevekovaya khudozhestvennaya rez'ba po derevu* (Medieval Georgian decorative wood-carving of the tenth and eleventh centuries). Tbilisi, 1958.

GABASHVILI, Ts. R. *Portalebi kartul arkitekturashi* (Portals in Georgian architecture). Tbilisi, 1955.

GAMSAKHURDIA, K. *The Hand of a Great Master*, trans. from the Georgian by Vakhtang Eristavi. Moscow, 1959.

GAPRINDASHVILI, G. *Peshcherny ansambl' Vardzia* (The cave complex of Vardzia). Tbilisi, 1960.

GARAQANIDZE, M. K. *Gruzinskoe derevyannoe zodchestvo* (Georgian architecture in wood). Tbilisi, 1959.

HASAN-I-RUMLU. *A chronicle of the early Safawis, being the Ahsanu't-Tawarikh*, trans. by C. N. Seddon. Baroda, 1934.

HILLS, D. C. *My Travels in Turkey*. London, 1964.

INGOROQVA, P. I. Lost Hymns of Georgia, in *UNESCO Courier*, May, 1962.

JAPARIDZE, V. V. *Gruzinskaya keramika* (Medieval Georgian ceramics). Tbilisi, 1956.

JOBADZE (DJOBADZE), V. Z. The Sculptures on the Eastern Façade of the Holy Cross of Mtzkhet'a, in *Oriens Christianus*, vols. 44–45. Wiesbaden, 1960–61.

KONDAKOV, N. P., and BAKRADZE, D. Z. *Opis' pamyatnikov drevnosti v nekotorykh khramakh i monastyryakh Gruzii* (Description of monuments of antiquity in Georgian cathedrals and monasteries). St Petersburg, 1890.

MSHVENIERADZE, D. M. *Gamokvabuli nagebobani Sakartveloshi* (Cave dwellings in Georgia), vol. 1. Tbilisi, 1955.

— *Stroitel'noe iskusstvo v drevnei Gruzii* (The art of building in ancient Georgia). Tbilisi, 1959.

SEVEROV, N. P., and CHUBIASHVILI, G. N. *Kumurdo i Nikordsminda* (Description of two important examples of Georgian church architecture). Moscow, 1947.

SHERVASHIDZE, L. A. *K voprosu o srednevekovoi gruzinskoi svetskoi miniatyure* (Georgian medieval secular minatures). Tbilisi, 1964.

SHMERLING, R. O. *Kartul khelnadserta mortulobis nimushebi* (Specimens of Georgian manuscript illuminations). Tbilisi, 1940.

— *Malye formy v arkhitekture srednevekovoi Gruzii* (Secondary features in Georgian medieval architecture). Tbilisi, 1962.

STESHENKO-KUFTINA, V. *Les plus anciens fondements instrumentaux de la musique populaire géorgienne. I. La flûte de Pan*. Tbilisi, 1936.

SUMBADZE, L. *Gruzinskie Darbazi* (The Georgian Darbazi house). Tbilisi, 1960.

TAQAISHVILI, E. S. Antiquities of Georgia, in *Georgica*, I, nos 4–5, London, 1937.

— *Arkheologicheskaya ekspeditsiya 1917-go goda v yuzhnye provintsii Gruzii* (The archaeological expedition of 1917 to the southern provinces of Georgia). Tbilisi, 1952.

— Four Basilican Churches of the Qvirila Valley, in *Georgica*, I, nos 2–3. London, 1936.

TSITSISHVILI, I. *Kartuli arkitekturis istoria* (History of Georgian architecture). Tbilisi, 1955.

VITRUVIUS. *De Architectura Libri Decem*, trans. by M. H. Morgan. Cambridge, Mass., 1914.

VOL'SKAYA, A. I. *Rel'efy Shiomgvime* (The bas-reliefs of Shio-Mghvime). Tbilisi, 1957.

CHAPTER VII

BARAMIDZE, A. G. *Narkvevebi kartuli literaturis istoriidan* (Studies in the history of Georgian literature). 4 vols., Tbilisi, 1940–64.

BOWRA, SIR MAURICE. *Inspiration and Poetry*, London, 1955. (Has a chapter on Rustaveli.)

GURGANI, FAKHR AL-DIN AS'AD. *Visramiani*. The Story of the Loves of Vis and Ramin. A romance of ancient Persia. Translated from the Georgian version by Oliver Wardrop. London, 1914.

JANELIDZE, D. *Gruzinsky teatr* (History of the early Georgian theatre). Tbilisi, 1959.

KARST, J. *Littérature géorgienne chrétienne*. Paris, 1934.

KEKELIDZE, K. S. *Etiudebi dzveli kartuli literaturis istoriidan* (Studies in the history of ancient Georgian literature). 9 vols., Tbilisi, 1945–63.

— *Kartuli literaturis istoria* (History of Georgian literature). New ed. 2 vols., Tbilisi, 1958–60.

LANG, D. M. *Lives and Legends of the Georgian Saints*. London, 1956.

— *The Wisdom of Balahvar: A Christian Legend of the Buddha*. London, 1957.

MOSES, OF KHONI. *Amiran-Darejaniani. A cycle of medieval Georgian tales . . .*, trans. by R. H. Stevenson. Oxford, 1958.

NUTSUBIDZE, S. *Istoriya gruzinskoi filosofii* (History of Georgian philosophy). Tbilisi, 1960.

RUSTAVELI, S. *Le Chevalier à la peau de tigre*, trans. by Serge Tsouladzé. Paris, 1964.

— *The Man in the Panther's Skin*, trans. by Marjory Scott Wardrop. London, 1912.

TARCHNISHVILI, M. *Geschichte der kirchlichen georgischen Literatur*. Vatican City, 1955.

TSERETELI, G. V. *The most ancient Georgian inscriptions from Palestine*. Tbilisi, 1960.

URUSHADZE, V. trans. *Anthology of Georgian Poetry*, 2nd ed. Tbilisi, 1958.

Sources of Illustrations

The great majority of the photographs were selected from the archives of the Institute of the History of Georgian Art, Tbilisi, and supplied by generous courtesy of the Deputy Director of the Institute, Professor Vakhtang Beridze, to whom thanks are expressed for his guidance and support in the preparation of this book. The photographs for plates 1, 2, 4, 5, 36 and 73 were kindly provided by Professor Hans Vogt, the well-known Caucasian scholar, Rector of the University of Oslo. The photograph of a painting by Lado Gudiashvili used in plate 3 was made available by Professor Shalva Amiranashvili, Director of the State Museum of Art, Tbilisi. For the photograph used in plate 8 I am indebted to the Director of the Barber Institute of Fine Arts, University of Birmingham. The photograph for plate 38 was taken on the spot by Professor Horace Gilbert of the California Institute of Technology, that for plate 50 by Mr David Winfield, of the Dumbarton Oaks Byzantine Centre. The fresco painting of Rustaveli reproduced in plate 71 was specially photographed at Jerusalem by Raphael Posener, and obtained for me by Professor Jonas Greenfield of the University of California, Berkeley. The miniatures shown in plate 72, a–d, are from coloured reproductions made by the Georgian State Museum. Mr John Webb photographed the coins shown in plate 74 from plaster casts specially made in the Coin Room of the British Museum.

Where not specifically acknowledged, the line drawings one taken from the latest Soviet field reports, kindly put at the author's disposal by the Georgian Academy of Sciences, Tbilisi.

The maps, figures 10, 16 and 21, were drawn by Mr H. A. Shelley. Figures 2, 6, 28, 35, 41–44 were drawn by Miss Gillian Jones.

Grateful acknowledgement is made to all the above-named.

THE PLATES

5

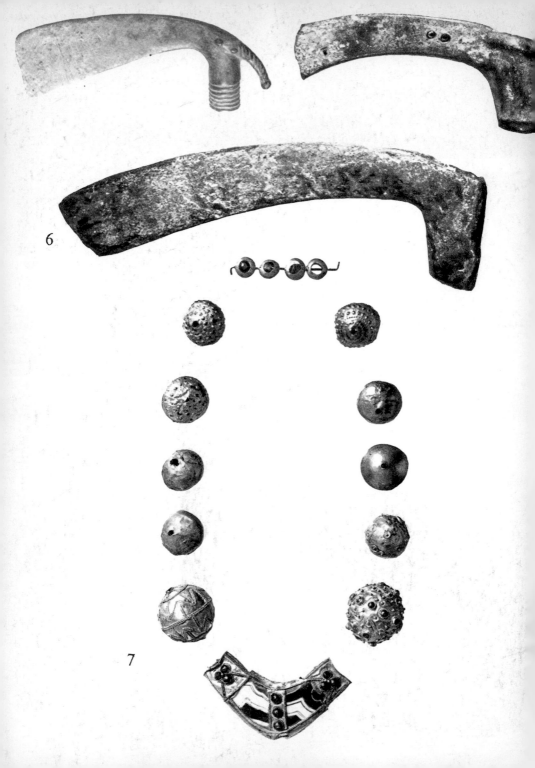

6

7

8

9

10

11

12

13

14

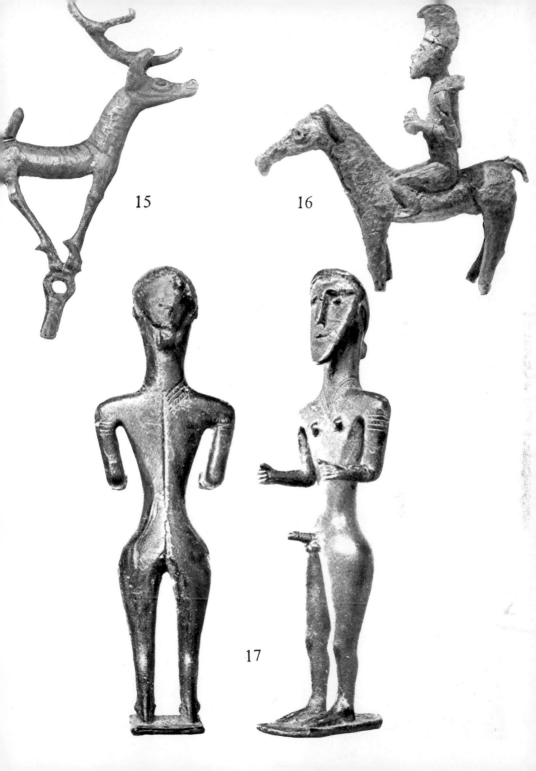

15

16

17

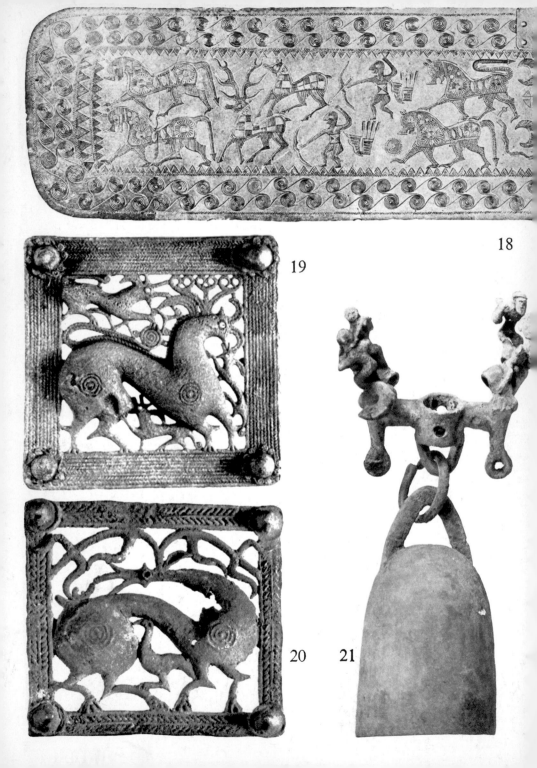

18

19

20

21

22   23

24

25

26

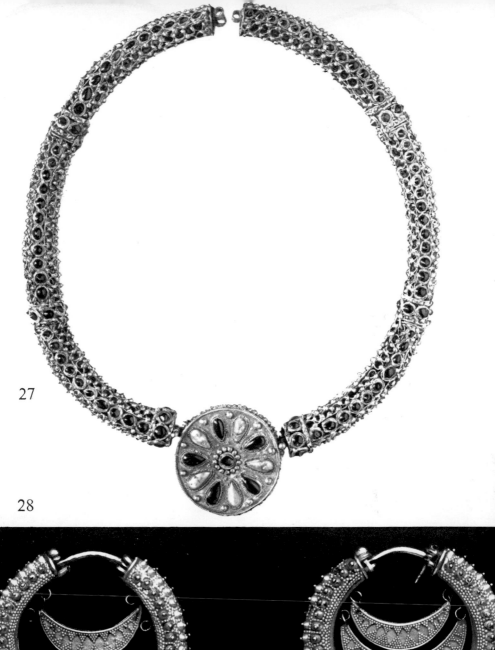

27

28

29

30

31

32

33

34

38

39

40

41

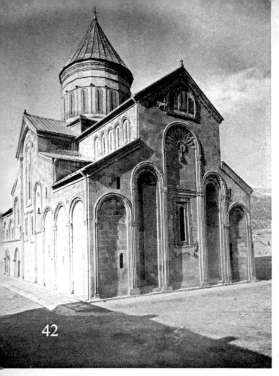

42

43

44

45

46

47

48

49

50

51

52

53

54

55

56

57

58

59

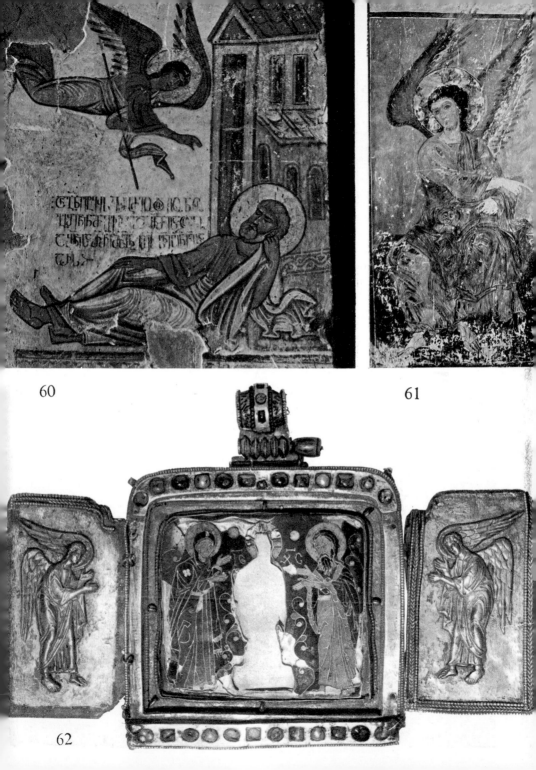

60

61

62

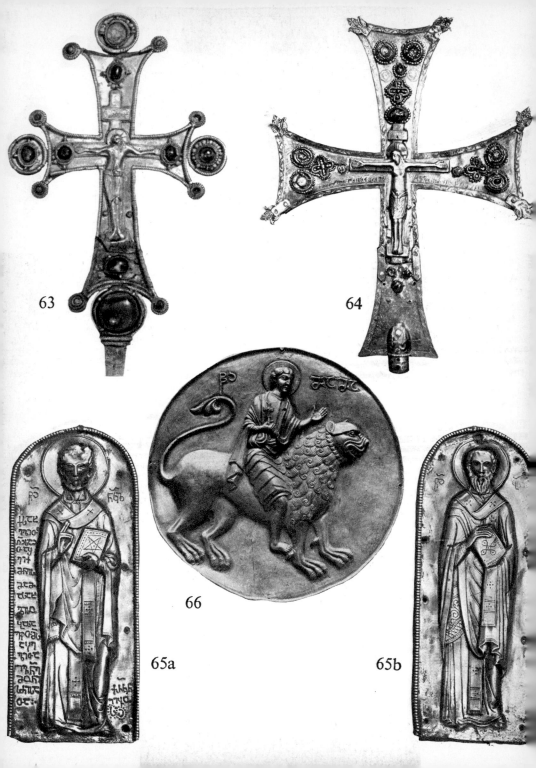

63

64

65a

66

65b

67

68

69

70

72

71

73

74

Notes on the Plates

1 General view of Mestia, the main township of the highland region of Svaneti in western Georgia. Note the characteristic stone watchtowers, with embrasures through which marauders could be shot down in the event of tribal raids. Photograph taken about 1890.

2 Medieval castle and modern village at Khertvisi, on the upper reaches of the River Mtkvari (Kura) in south-western Georgia. The fortifications shown in this picture, taken about 1890, date from the fourteenth century onwards, but Khertvisi has for two thousand years been a bastion protecting Georgia from invasion from the direction of Byzantium and Ottoman Turkey.

3 The carnival of *Qeenoba* in old Tbilisi, during the eighteenth century. From a painting by Lado Gudiashvili (b. 1896).

4 The beginning of collectivization in Georgian agriculture, about 1932. A collective vineyard in Kakheti. Note the small wheeled horse-ploughs, a modern development of the ancient ox-ploughs shown in fig. 17, and the characteristic black felt skull-caps worn by the farmers.

5 Peasant farmer in Imereti (western Georgia), about 1932. Beside him is an enormous wine jar, to be buried in the ground up to the neck. This jar is a direct descendant of the *pithoi* of ancient Colchian times, which were used as burial urns when no longer suitable for holding wine.

6 Bronze tube-socketed axeheads from Sachkhere, western Georgia. Early Bronze Age, *c*. 2200 BC. These axeheads range from 15 to 26 cm. long. State Museum of Georgia, Tbilisi.

7 Gold and jewelled necklace from Kurgan VIII, Trialeti. Middle Bronze Age, *c*. 1600 BC. Width of centrepiece 6.4 cm. State Museum of Georgia.

8 Jason taming the Bulls of Aeëtes, in the presence of Medea. Oil painting by Jean François de Troy (1679–1752). This is a sketch for one of the

seven large compositions illustrating the legend of Jason and the Argo-nauts, and the Golden Fleece, commissioned by the Manufacture des Gobelins in 1743. These sketches were executed in Rome, where de Troy was Director of the French Academy, and exhibited at the Louvre, Galerie d'Apollon, Salon of 1748. A set of the completed tapestries is in the Victoria and Albert Museum, London. Note the energetic treat-ment of the episode. The painting is also notable for its vivid colouring, and the imaginative reconstruction of the architecture of ancient Colchis. 21¾ in.× 50¾ in. Barber Institute of Fine Arts, University of Birmingham.

9   Gold goblet from Kurgan XVII, Trialeti, of unalloyed metal, decorated with granulation, appliqué and filigree work, and inlaid with sardonyx, coloured glass paste, and, on the base, amber. Middle Bronze Age, *c.* 1500 BC. Height 8 cm. State Museum of Georgia.

10   Gold ferrule of a ceremonial funerary standard from Kurgan XV of the Trialeti burial grounds, showing a pattern of rampant lions in the upper register, and a Greek key pattern in the lower.

11   Chased silver goblet from Kurgan V, Trialeti. The upper register shows a ritual procession of hierophants wearing animal masks, reflecting Ana-tolian cult influences, and the lower register a procession of sacrificial animals. Out of sight, on the other side of the upper register, is a figure, evidently a high priest, seated on a throne beside a sacred tree, perhaps the Tree of Life, with a pedestal vase, an altar and guardian animals near by. About 1500 BC. Height 11 cm. State Museum of Georgia.

12   Bronze axehead, engraved with stylized animal figure and linear patterns, from Tskhinvali, South Ossetia. Eighth century BC. Length 17 cm. State Museum of Georgia.

13   Late Bronze Age battle-axe from Akhalkalaki, south-western Georgia, *c.* 1200 BC. Width of blade about 10 cm. State Museum of Georgia.

14   Black burnished clay *pithos* from Kurgan XVII, Trialeti, the neck decorated with swastika patterns. Middle Bronze Age. Height 51 cm. State Museum of Georgia.

15 Bronze standard-head in the form of a stag, from Ratcha district; of great interest as an echo of the well-known standard-heads from Alaca Hüyük. Western Georgian. *c.* 900 BC. State Museum of Georgia.

16 Bronze model of a horseman, wearing a Phrygian style crested helmet. From Tsageri, western Georgia. *c.* 1000 BC. Tsageri District Museum.

17 Ithyphallic bronze male figure from Zekari, *c.* 750 BC. Height 25 cm. Kutaisi Historical and Ethnographic Museum.

18 Bronze girdle plate depicting hunting scene, from Burial No. 5 at Maral-Deresi, Trialeti. This example has been dated variously, some authorities assigning it to *c.* 1500 BC, though the State Museum of Georgia now assigns it to the ninth century BC. Among the animals shown are stags, a fish, two antelopes, two horses, a boar, and does, as well as six mythical beasts with clawed feet. Note the lunar symbols on the horses' heads. 98×21 cm. State Museum of Georgia.

19 Bronze belt buckle, showing a combination of Scythian-style animal figures, with bosses at the corners. From the Ratcha district of western Georgia. 13.2 cm. square. First century AD.

20 Another example of a Georgian bronze belt buckle, showing a different and more fantastic treatment of the animal motif. From Ratcha district. First century BC. 9.8×9.3 cm. State Museum of Art, Tbilisi.

21 Bronze standard terminal with bell attached, from the Kazbek or Stepan-dsminda hoard, sixth century BC. The left-hand fork has two human figures locked in combat, probably wrestling, while the right-hand fork is surmounted by a warrior with a shield riding on the back of another man. State Museum of Georgia.

22 Another bronze standard terminal from the Kazbek hoard, sixth century BC. The multiplicity of bull's horns points to some bovine cult, with probable links with ancient bull cults of Anatolia. See James Mellaart, *Earliest Civilizations of the Near East*, pp. 97–101, citing examples from Çatal Hüyük dating back as far as 6000 BC. State Museum of Georgia.

23 One of a set of four silver-sheathed legs of a funerary couch from the Bagineti sarcophagus at Mtskheta-Armazi, ancient capital of the Iberian kings. Second century AD. State Museum of Georgia.

24 Oval cameo pendant on a gold chain, showing a dog, mounted in gold and almandine, with three pearls suspended on gold wire. Length of chain 47 cm.; size of cameo 2·4×1·9 cm. From Burial-chamber No. 2, Armazis-Khevi, end of second century AD. State Museum of Georgia.

25 Gold necklace with circular gold locket, set with an amethyst ram's head surrounded by cabochon almandines and turquoises. Suspended from the necklace by a gold chain is a small phial for holding aromatic balsams, also inset with almandines and turquoise. Over-all length of necklace 23 cm.; diameter of locket 4·2 cm. From female Burial-chamber No. 7, Armazis-Khevi, late second century AD. State Museum of Georgia.

26 Convex oval garnet intaglio, forming the centre-piece of a rectangular granulated gold brooch or belt ornament, and depicting the Eristav or Pitiakhsh Zevakh, a grandee of the Iberian court, with his wife Karpak, according to the Greek marginal legend. From Burial-chamber No. 1, Armazis-Khevi. State Museum of Georgia.

27 Golden *à jour* necklet, with granulated locket inset with almandines and turquoises, from female Burial-chamber No. 7, late second century AD. Each arc of the necklet is 30 cm. long; diameter of the locket 5 cm. Total weight of the ensemble 180 gr. State Museum of Georgia.

28 Pair of gold earrings from the so-called Akhalgori hoard, fifth century BC. 5·6×5·2 cm. Further examples from this superb find of gold ornaments and plate, reflecting a blend of Achaemenid and local Georgian inspiration, are illustrated in Tamara Talbot Rice, *Ancient Arts of Central Asia*, Ill. 11 and 12. State Museum of Georgia.

29 Epitaph of Princess Serapita, in Greek, and Middle Persian in 'Armazi' script, from Burial-chamber No. 4 at Armazis-Khevi. Mid-second century AD. 1·93×0·65 m. State Museum of Georgia.

30 Roman-style mausoleum, discovered in 1951 close to Mtskheta railway station. First century AD.

31 General view of the cave-city of Uplistsikhe, in Kartli, one of the most ancient urban centres of Bronze Age and Classical Iberia.

32 Interior of an underground chamber in the cave-city of Uplistsikhe. First or second century AD.

33 Bolnisi Sioni, an important basilican church in Kartli province, built between 478 and 493. Wall inscription recording the completion of the edifice. One of the most ancient examples of the Georgian *Khutsuri* or ecclesiastical script, in its uncial form.

34 General view of Bolnisi Sioni.

35 Interior brick-vaulting of Bolnisi Sioni, end of fifth century AD.

36 The Elevation of the Cross. Tympanum of the south door of the church of Jvari, or the Holy Cross, on a high hill overlooking Mtskheta and the confluence of the Aragvi and Mtkvari (Kura) rivers. *c.* AD 600.

37 Old Shuamta, in Kakheti. Monastic ensemble showing the fifth-century basilica and two cruciform churches of the seventh century.

38 Southern façade of the Jvari church, near Mtskheta. The ground plan is in the form of an apsed square with miniature apses in the diagonals and then four square chapels at the corners, producing an interior of great spatial complexity. The eastern façade (not shown here) is sculpted with reliefs portraying the contemporary princes of Iberia.

39 View from the south-west of the double-domed basilican church of All Saints at Gurjaani, in Kakheti province, Eastern Georgia. Eighth century.

40 Seventh-century basilica at Dmanisi, once an important trading centre, situated in Kartli, about 100 km. south-west of Tbilisi. The small

chapel to the right, on the west side, was added between 1213 and 1223, in the reign of King Giorgi Lasha.

41 Kumurdo church, near Akhalkalaki, in the Javakheti region of south-western Georgia. Built in 964 by the architect Sakotsari. Part of the eastern façade. This famous church, built of rose-coloured stone, is characterized by the high quality of the masonry work.

42 Patriarchal cathedral of Sveti-tskhoveli (the Life-Giving Pillar) at Mtskheta, erected by the architect Constantine Arsukidze (Arsakidze) between 1010 and 1029. General view from south-east.

43 Cathedral of Allaverdi in Kakheti, general view from the north-west. First quarter of the eleventh century. Note the lofty drum, which produces a magnificent effect when viewed against the Caucasus mountain range to the north.

44 Cathedral of Samtavisi, in Kartli province, built in 1030 under the direction of Bishop Ilarion of Samtavisi. General view from the north-east, showing the free-standing belfry, evidently of later date. This cathedral is noteworthy for its elegant and graceful proportions, and for the harmonious geometrical patterns and stone interlace work on the façades and window-surrounds.

45 Ruins of the Bagrat cathedral at Kutaisi, the ancient capital of western Georgia, formerly Aea. Built in 1003, it was blown up by the Turks in 1691.

46 Pair of fantastic birds, carved in stone on the south chapel of the church at Nikordsminda in Ratcha district, western Georgia. AD 1010–14.

47 Part of the eastern façade of Nikordsminda church, showing a pair of warrior saints, and other sacred figures.

48 East window of Savane church in Imereti, western Georgia. Built by the architect Arabay in 1046.

49 Samtavro church at Mtskheta, decoration of the south windows. First half of the eleventh century.

50 Sculptured capital from the church at Oshki in Tao province, now within Turkey. Figure of an angel. As David Winfield has pointed out, the rich figure sculptures on this great church, built between 958 and 966, anticipate to a remarkable degree the carvings on European Romanesque churches of succeeding centuries.

51 Detail of carved interlace work from a window at Kvatakhevi monastery church, in Kartli province. Late twelfth century.

52 View from the south-east of the monastery and cathedral at Gelati, near Kutaisi, in western Georgia. Founded in 1106 by King David the Builder.

53 Ruins of the medieval academy and university of Iqalto, in Kakheti, eastern Georgia. This celebrated seat of learning reached international eminence during the twelfth century, its most eminent rector being the philosopher Arsen Iqaltoeli.

54 Fortified tower at the monastery of Ubisi, in Imereti, built in 1141. The church is renowned for its magnificent fresco paintings.

55 View of the cave monastery of Vardzia, constructed towards the end of the twelfth century. The cells, halls, store-rooms, chapels and public rooms are cut out of solid rock in a lofty cliff in the upper Mtkvari valley, close to the modern Turkish frontier. The monastery was sacked and destroyed by the Persian Shah Tahmasp in the sixteenth century.

56 Vardzia: interior of the principal church, carved out of solid rock. Fresco paintings of King Giorgi III (1156–84) and his daughter Queen Tamar (1184–1213) are seen on the left of the photograph.

57 Geguti, near Kutaisi, in Imereti (western Georgia). Ruins of the twelfth-century royal palace.

58 Carved wooden door from Chukuli, in highland Svaneti. Eleventh century. Height 1·61 m.

59 Carved wooden door from Jakhunderi, Svaneti. Eleventh century. Height 1·59 m.

60 The angel appears to Joseph, husband of Mary, to give him warning of the birth of Christ. Fresco in the church at Ateni, Kartli province. Tenth century.

61 Figure of an angel, from a fresco painting of the Resurrection at Qindsvisi church. About 1200.

62 Jewelled and enamelled triptych from Martvili monastery. Usually assigned to the eighth or ninth century. The central panel has retained its brilliant colouring in blues, purple and red on a green background. Central panel 12·2 cm. square. State Museum of Art, Tbilisi.

63 Jewelled processional cross of King David the Builder (1089–1125) 24×17 cm. State Museum of Art, Tbilisi.

64 Jewelled processional cross from the Ishkhani monastery in south-western Georgia, now within Turkey. AD 973. 51×36 cm. State Museum of Art, Tbilisi.

65 Two small repoussé plaques from the Icon of the Virgin from Shemok-medi monastery, Guria: (a) St Nicholas; (b) St Basil. Made by the master Ivane Monisdze, AD 1040. State Museum of Art, Tbilisi.

66 Silver roundel portraying St Mamay riding upon a lion, from the Gelati monastery. V. V. Beridze assigns this to the eleventh century, though Shalva Amiranashvili (*Istoriya gruzinskogo iskusstva*, pp. 124–27) considers it more typical of the sixth to seventh centuries. Diameter 20·5 cm. State Museum of Art, Tbilisi.

67 Silver repoussé plaque from Sagolasheni, showing the Annunciation. *c.* AD 1000. 30·2×34·3 cm. State Museum of Art, Tbilisi.

68 Part of the cover of the Berta Gospels, made by the master goldsmith

Beshken Opizari. Twelfth century. Institute of Manuscripts of the Academy of Sciences, Tbilisi.

69 Detail from the central panel of the jewelled and enamelled gold icon of the Khakhuli Virgin, from the Gelati monastery. Coloured reproductions of the triptych are given in Tamara Talbot Rice, *Ancient Arts of Central Asia*, Ill. 241, 242. This superb masterpiece, richly studded with precious stones and cloisonné enamel miniatures, was in process of creation and embellishment by a succession of masters, from the tenth to the twelfth century. State Museum of Art, Tbilisi.

70 Icon of the Laklakidze family. Detail of the border, showing Christ's entry into Jerusalem. Eleventh century. Width 64 cm. State Museum of Art, Tbilisi.

71 Coloured fresco showing the Georgian national poet, Shota Rustaveli (born *c.* 1166), in court robes in pose of adoration. From the former Georgian Monastery of the Cross, Jerusalem (now incorporated in the Greek Patriarchate), where Rustaveli is traditionally supposed to have finished his life as a monk.

72 Seventeenth-century miniatures, showing scenes from Rustaveli's epic, *Vepkhistqaosani* or 'The Man in the Panther's Skin'—the hunt of King Rostevan, Tariel sitting by the brook, etc. Note the strong Persian influence, reflecting the popularity in Georgia of epics such as Firdawsi's *Shah-Nameh*, and the influence of Safavi art generally. From MS. No. 5006 of the Institute of Manuscripts, Tbilisi, dating from the seventeenth century. Size of each painting about 13 × 17 cm.

73 Leo. One of a set of miniatures showing the Signs of the Zodiac, from an astronomical and astrological treatise copied in AD 1188, No. 65 of the Institute of Manuscripts, Tbilisi (formerly in the Ecclesiastical Museum Collection).

74 Coins of Colchis, Iberia and Georgia, from about 500 BC to AD 1247. All the specimens illustrated are in the collection of the British Museum and are reproduced by courtesy of the Trustees and the Keeper of the Department of Coins and Medals, Mr G. K. Jenkins.

(a) Silver didrachm of Colchis, 500 BC or later. *Obv.* Crouching (hermaphrodite) lion, to left, with head turned back. Long mane, prominent teats. *Rev.* Kneeling human figure, with bull's head, resembling a minotaur, in oblong incuse. Collar around neck.

(b) Silver hemidrachm of Colchis, 400 BC or later. A very common coin in wide circulation. *Obv.* Female head, facing right, of archaic style. Hair falls in three tresses down the back of the neck. Various suggestions have been made concerning the identity of this figure, for instance that it represents the legendary sorceress Medea, or else the wood goddess Dali, whose cult corresponds to that of Artemis. *Rev.* Bull's head, facing right. The bull played a central part in the ancient Anatolian and Caucasian mythology and economy.

(c) Silver tetradrachm of Colchis. About 400 BC. A very rare piece. *Obv.* Lion's head, facing left, with mouth open, showing fangs and tongue. *Rev.* Forepart of a winged Pegasus, to right, in square incuse.

(d) Silver coin of Aristarchus, dynast of Colchis under Pompey (*c.* 63–47 BC). *Obv.* Head of Pompey, facing right. *Rev.* Seated female figure, Tyche.

(e) Bronze coin of Dioscurias, an important Greek settlement on the Black Sea coast of Abkhazia, the modern Sukhumi. *c.* 100 BC. *Obv.* Caps of the Dioscuri, Castor and Pollux, surmounted by six-pointed stars. *Rev.* Name of the city in Greek characters, with thyrsos.

(f) Silver drachm of Duke Stephen of Iberia, *c.* AD 600. Copied from the coinage of the Sasanian king Hormizd IV (AD 579–90), but with Christian symbolism indicating aspirations towards independence. *Obv.* Bust of Hormizd, facing right, with name of Duke Stephen in Georgian ecclesiastical characters. *Rev.* Zoroastrian fire-altar, surmounted with Christian cross.

(g) Silver coin of King Giorgi II (1072–89). *Obv.* Facing figure of the Blachernae Virgin. *Rev.* Pious invocation, incorporating the king's Byzantine title of Caesar.

(h) Unique copper coin of King David the Builder (1089–1125), presented to the British Museum by the Earl of Enniskillen in 1857. *Obv.* King David, facing, holding emblems of royalty. *Rev.* Maltese Cross, surrounded by titles of King David, as ruler of the Abkhazians, Kartlians, Kakhetians, Ranians and Armenians.

(i) Copper coin of King Giorgi III (1156–84). AD 1174. *Obv.* King seated cross-legged in oriental fashion, facing. On his uplifted right hand sits a falcon. *Rev.* Arabic inscription: 'King of Kings, Giorgi son of Dimitri, Sword of the Messiah'.

(j) Irregular cast planchet, of Queen Tamar (1184–1213). These pieces are rough lumps of copper, struck with the coin die, often in several places, and then authenticated with various counterstamps. The obverse alone is shown. In the centre of the die is the monogram of Queen Tamar formed of interlaced Georgian *mkhedruli* or 'knightly' letters. There are two counterstamps, one in the form of the Georgian letter 'D' in an oblong incuse, with a dot in the middle. These coins were struck in haste in great abundance for use in the territories temporarily occupied by Georgian troops.

(k) Copper coin struck jointly in the names of Queen Tamar and her father, King Giorgi III, who admitted her to co-regnancy in 1178. *Obv.* 'GI', for Giorgi, with ornamental border. *Rev.* 'TR', for Tamar, with ornamental border.

(l) Copper coin of regular fabric, struck jointly in the names of Tamar and her second husband, David Soslan. AD 1200. *Obv.* Bagratid royal emblem in the form of a standard, with initials of rulers. *Rev.* 'Queen of Queens, Glory of the World and Faith, Tamar, daughter of Giorgi, Champion of the Messiah'.

(m) Regular copper of Tamar's son, Giorgi Lasha (1213–23). During this reign, the Mongols first made their appearance in the Caucasus region.

(n) Silver dirhem of Queen Rusudan, daughter of Queen Tamar. AD 1230. *Obv.* Bust of Christ, bearded, facing, head and shoulders length, mantle and nimbus. Right hand in blessing, left holding Book of Gospels, with three pellets on cover. *Rev.* Georgian uncials 'RSN', for Rusudan, surrounded by Arabic legend: 'Queen of Queens, Glory of the World and Faith, Rusudan, daughter of Tamar, Champion of the Messiah'.

(o) Silver dirhem of King David Narin, a Georgian vassal of the Supreme Khan of the Mongols. AD 1247. *Obv.* The king on horseback, to right, with royal monogram 'DT' for Davit. *Rev.* 'By the power of God, King David, slave of the dominion of the Great Khan Kuyuk'.

Index

Abasgia, *see* Abkhazia
'Abbas I, shah of Iran, 17
Abbevillian culture, 30
Abesadze, Ts. N., Georgian archaeologist, 40
Abesalom and Eteri, 169
Abibos, Saint, of Nekresi, 97
Abkhaz, Abkhazia, 20, 24, 30–1, 34, 36, 42, 51, 70–2, 89, 94, 108, 112, 166
Abo, Saint and Martyr, of Tbilisi, 156
Abrskil, legend of, 70–1
Acheulian culture, 30–1
Adarnase IV, king of the Georgians, 107
Adsquri, 124
Aeëtes, king of Colchis, 64, 68–9, 80, 112
Aeschylus, 70
Agathias of Myrina, 100
Ahura-Mazda, 88
Ajaria (Atchara), 20, 59, 77
Akhalgori hoard, 83
Akhalkalaki, 111
Akhaltsikhe, 37, 177
Alaca Hüyük burials, 44
Alans, 20, 86
Alarodians, tribe, 74
Alazani, river, 78, 90, 136
Albania, Caucasian, 17–18, 80, 83, 90, 98, 153
Albright, W. F., 38, 50
Alexander the Great, 81, 83–4, 126
Alexander I, tsar of Russia, 106
Alexius Komnenos, 115
Allaverdi cathedral, 134, 136
Allen, W. E. D., 116
Alp Arslan, Seljuk sultan, 111, 158
Ambaris, king of Tabal, 56
Amilakhvari family, 116
Amiran, legend of, 70–1

Amiran-Darejaniani, 168–9
Amiran, Ruth, 38
Amiranashvili, Shalva Ia., 60, 140, 142
Amiranis-gora, Chalcolithic settlement, 37–39
Amirejibi family, 116
Amisus, 80
Anaklia, Neolithic settlement at, 34
Ananuri, 124
Anatolia, 19–20, 24, 34, 38–9, 43–4, 50, 52–57, 66, 72–4, 81–3, 87, 90, 95, 110
Anchi, icon of, 141
Andrew, Saint and Apostle, 166
Ani, 110, 112
Antioch, 98, 159, 166
Antoni I, Georgian Patriarch, 172
Apakidze, Professor Andria, 83
apes, anthropoid, remains found in Georgia, 29
Apollo, 89–90
Apollonius Rhodius, 65–9
Arabs, Arabic, 20, 23, 101–5, 107, 110, 159
Aragvi, river, 60, 78, 82
Araqishvili, Dimitri, Georgian composer, 115
Ararat, Mount, 52
Araxes, river, 44
Ardahan, 20, 110
Argishti, king of Urartu, 58
Argonauts, 64–9
Argveti, province, 111
Aristarchus, dynast of Colchis, 82
Armazi, pagan deity, 88; script, 152–3
Armaz-tsikhe (Harmozika), 78, 82, 89, 103, 123
Armenia, Armenians, 17–19, 24, 28, 30, 39–40, 50, 53–4, 60, 74–6, 80, 83–6, 91, 94, 97–8, 101, 103, 105–8, 110, 112, 129–131, 137, 142–3, 148, 150, 153–5, 158

Arsacid dynasty, 86, 95
Arsen of Iqalto, 167
Arsenius II, Georgian Patriarch, 156
Arsukidze, master-builder Constantine, 134–135
Artag, Iberian king, 86
Artanuji, 105
Artemis, 88
Ashot the Great, Kuropalates, 105, 131
Asia, king of the Daiaeni, 58
Asia Minor, *see* Anatolia
Asparukh, Iberian viceroy, 85, 87
Assyria, Assyrians, 20, 54–60, 73, 87, 112
Ateni church, 140
Athos, Mount, 107–8, 149, 159, 165–6
Augustus, Roman emperor, 81, 95
Aurignacian culture in Georgia, 30, 33
Avars, tribe, 24
Azerbaijan, 17–18, 36, 60, 83, 115

Babylonia, 66, 87
Baghdad, 103, 156, 159
Bagineti, Mount, 82
Bagrat, Eristavi-of-Eristavis, 132
Bagrat III, king of Georgia, 108–9, 133–4
Bagrat IV, king of Georgia, 110–11
Bagratid dynasty, 105–18, 130, 158
Bagvashi, Liparit, 111
Bagvashi, Rati, 109
Baku, 72
Bakur, prince, 91
Bal'mont, Constantine, 173
Baltrušaitis, Jurgis, 138
Bana church, 130
Bardas Phocas, 108
Bardas Scleros, 107–9
Basil II, Byzantine emperor, 107–10
Basque language, 18, 77
Batumi, 20, 64, 67, 75, 99
Bayburt, 20, 106
Berdzenishvili (Kiladze), N.Z., Soviet archaeologist, 30, 33
Beshkenid dynasty, 115
Bethlehem, 98, 154, 159

Bichvinta (Pitiunt, Pitsunda), 64, 94
Black Sea, 17, 20, 22, 30, 34, 39, 55, 59, 64–69, 72, 77, 80, 94, 99, 114, 119, 124
Bodbe, tomb of Saint Nino, 94
Bogolyubskoi, Georgy, 114
Bolnisi cathedral, 128, 154
Borjomi, 50
Bronze Age metallurgy in Georgia, 39–53
Buddha, 159–65
Bulgarians, Bulgaria, 109–10, 159, 171
Buxton, David Roden, 129, 138
Buzmihr the *pitiakhsh*, 89
Byzantine empire, 81, 96, 99–103, 105–11, 114, 137, 141–4, 149–50, 152–3, 169–71

Caspian Sea, 68, 72, 80
Catharine, monastery of Saint, 109, 150
cattle-raising in Georgia, 35, 37, 45
Caucasian languages, 22–7
Chakhrukhadze, 167
Chalcedon, Council of, 98, 159
Chalcolithic culture in Georgia, 33, 36–41
Chalybes, tribe, 50, 66, 75
Chantre, E., 60
Checheno-Ingush tribe, 24, 39, 77
Chellean culture, 30
Chiatura district, 32
Chikovani, Prof. M., 169
Childe, Prof. V. Gordon, 38, 49
China, Chinese porcelain, 143, 145–6, 149–150
Chordvaneli, John-Varazvache, 107–8
Chorokhi, river, 20, 67, 76, 106
Chosroid dynasty, 95–6
Christianity, adopted in Georgia, 91–5
chronology, system of Georgian, 106–7
Chubinishvili, Tariel, Soviet archaeologist, 36–7, 39
Cimmerians, 20, 56, 72–3, 82
Circassians, 20, 24, 77
climatic conditions in Georgia, 22
coinage, origins of in Georgia, 80–1
Colchis, 23, 31, 34, 59–70, 72–7, 79–82, 89, 94, 99, 108, 120, 152

Constantine the Great, 91
Constantine Porphyrogenitus, emperor, 106
Constantine VIII, emperor, 107–8
Constantine Monomachus, emperor, 110
Constantinople, 98, 114, 138, 142, 166, 170, 178
Crimea, 34, 51, 80
Crusaders, 96, 111, 114
Cyprus, 159

Dablagomi, Eneolithic finds from, 38
Daghestan, 24, 36, 39, 77, 104, 112, 124, 136
Dali, Georgian wood goddess, 80, 88
darbazi house, 119–23
Darius, king of Iran, 74
Daryal Pass, 72, 86
David, Saint, of Garesja, 128, 157
David, king of Israel, 105, 158
David the Builder, king of Georgia, 104, 111–12, 136, 167, 171
David Soslan, 114, 150, 167
David the Great, Kuropalates, 108–9
Deeters, Prof. G., 77
Derbent, 72, 112
Devis-Khvreli, Aurignacian cave camp at, 33
Diauehi (Daiaeni), 57–9, 74–6, 82
Dimitri I, king of Georgia, 104–5
Dionysius the Areopagite, 98, 159, 167
Dioscurias (Sukhumi), 20, 30, 51, 64, 76, 79–81
Dmanisi, 142, 144
Dodo, Saint, 128
dolmens, 42
Dorotheus I, Patriarch of Jerusalem, 113
Dsqaldsitela, river, 30, 137
Dsromi, church at, 130
Dvin, synod at, 98
Dzevri, Palaeolithic finds from, 33

Echmiadzin, 129
Egypt, 73, 85, 102, 113, 143, 148, 156
Elbruz, Mount, 64, 68, 75
Ephrem Mtsire, 167

Erekle II, king of Georgia, 178
Eristavi family, 116
Erzerum, 20, 103, 106
Esheri, dolmen complex at, 51
Euphrates, river, 55
Eustace, Saint, of Mtskheta, 100, 154
Eustace Placidus, Saint, 139
Euthymius the Iberian, Saint, 107–8, 160, 165–7
Ezechiel, the Prophet, 56–7, 73

Farsman (Farasmanes), king of Iberia, 87, 152
Fereidan, Georgians at, 17
feudal system in Georgia, 96–7, 116–18
Foley, Tom, 161
Forbes, R. J., 41, 50, 67
Frankfort, Henri, 49
Frierman, Jay D., 142–9

Gabashvili, E. G., Soviet geologist, 29
Gagra, 30
Gaiane, Saint, 94
Gaim, pagan idol, 88
Galilee, Sea of, 38
Gamsakhurdia, Konstantine, 135
Ganja, 50
Gaprindashvili, Givi, 158
Garesja, 29
Gasgas (Kashki), 55
Gatsi, pagan idol, 88
Gebi, Bronze Age mining centre, 50
Geguti, palace at, 123
Gelati, cathedral, monastery and academy, 112, 134, 136–7, 141, 171
Genesis, Book of, 56–7, 157
George, Saint, 18, 90, 112, 136
George the Hagiorite, Saint, 108, 165–6
Georgian language, 25–7
Gimbutas, M., 36, 43
Giorgi I, king of Georgia, 110, 135
Giorgi II, king of Georgia, 111
Giorgi III, king of Georgia, 114, 174
Giorgi IV Lasha, king of Georgia, 114

Giorgi Merchule, 109, 131, 157
Gog and Magog, 56–7, 73
Gogarene, province, 75
Golden Fleece, legend, 64–9
Gomer, *see* Cimmerians
Gori, 50, 82
Greece, Greeks, 19–20, 56, 64, 67–8, 76,
    79–80, 84–6, 89–90, 101, 107, 109–11,
    142, 150, 152–3, 160
Gregory, Saint, the Illuminator, 91, 94
Gregory of Khandzta, Saint, 105, 109, 131,
    149, 157
Gremi, 124
Grigol Bakurianisdze, 171
Guaram, prince of Iberia, 100
Gubaz II, king of Lazica, 100
Gudarekhi, pottery-making at, 144
Gudauti, 34, 51
Gurgani, Fakhr-al-Din, 168
Gurgen II, Georgian king, 109
Guria, 59, 77, 119, 150
Gurjaani, basilica at, 128
Gvarjilasklde, Magdalenian culture remains
    found at, 32

Hadas, Moses, 65
Hadrian, Roman emperor, 86
Halys, river, 56
Hančar, F., 60
Harmozika, *see* Armaz-tsikhe
Hasan-i-Rumlu, Persian chronicler, 126–7
Hattusilis III, king of the Hittites, 66
Heniochi, pirate tribe, 20, 69–70, 85
Heraclius, Byzantine emperor, 101–2, 110
Herodotus, 18, 66–7, 72, 74
Hills, D. C., 67, 133
Hittites, 19–20, 44, 52–3, 66, 72, 87
Homer, 65
Hormizd IV, king of Iran, 100
Horoztepe, burials at, 44
Hurrians, 19, 24, 39, 52, 74

Iberia, Caucasian, 18, 22, 57, 75–6, 80, 82–
    96, 103, 153

Ibn al-Azraq, 104
Iese of Dsilkani, Saint, 156
Ildamusha, Colchian city, 59
Imereti, 22–3, 32–3, 36, 50, 59, 75, 106, 112,
    134
Inaishvili, A., 99
Indo-Europeans, 23–5, 43–4, 72, 74, 82
Ingoroqva, P., 150
Inguri, river, 30
Ioane Mtbevari, 149
Ioane Sabanisdze, 103, 156
Ioane Zedazneli, Saint, 156
Iodmangan, master of the court, 152
Iqalto, 136, 144, 167
Iran, Iranians, 17, 20, 34, 43–4, 49, 74, 76,
    83, 86–7, 90, 95–7, 99–103, 112, 115,
    118, 142–3, 149, 152, 155, 158, 169, 174,
    176–8
Iraq, 34
iron and steel, 66
Isfahan, 17, 94
Ispir, 76, 106
Israel, 73, 105
Italos, Johannes, 170
ithyphallic figures, 63–4
Ivashchenko, M. M., Soviet archaeologist,
    44, 79
Iviron monastery, 107–8, 165–6

Jacob of Tsurtavi, 154–5
Jacques de Vitry, Patriarch of Jerusalem, 112
Jafarid amirs, 104
Japaridze, Otar, Georgian archaeologist, 39–
    40
Japaridze, V. V., Georgian archaeologist,
    142, 148
Japhetic theory, 24–5, 77
Jason, 64–9, 84
Javakheti province, 60, 75, 109–10, 122
Jedlička, J., 173
Jerusalem, 101, 111–12, 159, 167, 173
Jews, 86, 94, 101, 104
Jibghu, Khazar khaqan, 101–2
Jobadze, V., art historian, 130

John Chrysostom, Saint, 167
John Damascene, Saint, 167
Juansher, history of, 157, 159
Julfa, New, 94
Justinian, Byzantine emperor, 88, 100
Jvari church, near Mtskheta, 101, 129

Kabardians, 24, 70
Kakheti province, 19, 23, 60, 63–4, 75, 90, 94, 100, 109, 123–4, 128, 134, 136, 157, 167
Kalandadze, A. N., Georgian archaeologist, 34–5
Kars, 20
Kartli province, 18–19, 22–3, 31, 37, 39, 42, 60, 75, 100, 103, 108, 111, 122, 154
Kartlis tskhovreba, chronicle, 83, 88, 159
Kartlos, supposed ancestor of Georgians, 18, 84
kartvelebi, local name of Georgians, 17
Katskhi church, 139
Kayakent, 36
Kazbek, Mount, 63, 72, 129
Kazvin, 115
Kenyon, Kathleen, 38
Kephalari, 47
Kernd'l, A., 31
Khakhani, Colchian king, 59
Khakhuli (Haho) church, 132–3, 141
Khaldi, Urartian god, 59
Khazars, 101–2, 156
Khertvisi, 124
Khevsurs, Georgian mountain tribe, 64, 96
Khirbet Kerak pottery, 38–9
Khizaant-gora, 40
Khrami, river, 31, 44
Khushalkhi, 59
Khusrau Anushirvan, king of Iran, 99–100
Khwarazm, Khwarazmians, 178
Kiladze, N. Z., *see* Berdzenishvili
Kirovakan, Armenian *kurgan* site, 50
Kistrika, 34
Kizzuwatna, 66
Klarjeti, province, 109, 130–1, 141

Klimov, G. A., Soviet linguist, 77–8
Koban-Colchian culture, 60–3
Kola, 97, 110
Kosven, M. O., Soviet anthropologist, 33
Ksani, river, 83
Ksefarnug, Iberian king, 87, 152
Kuban, river, 43
Kudaro, Palaeolithic remains from, 31
Kuftin, B. A., Soviet archaeologist, 44, 69
Kuji, king of Colchis, 84
Kül-Tepe, excavations at, 37, 40
Kulbakebi, Chalcolithic site, 39–40
Kura, river, *see* Mtkvari
Kuro-Araxes culture, 36–41
Kutaisi (Aea), 33–4, 64, 68, 78, 112, 123, 134, 142
Kvatskhelebi, excavations at, 37, 40

La Tène culture, 45
Lachish, pottery from, 38
Lashe-Balta, Palaeolithic remains from, 31
Laz, Lazica, Lazistan, 19–20, 22–3, 66–7, 75, 77, 81, 94, 99–100, 108, 152
Lechkhumi district, 75
Leonti Mroveli, medieval chronicler, 158–9
Leucothea, sun goddess, 89
Lezghians, tribe, 24
Lucian, hermit, 157
Luristan, 147
Lysimachus, 81
Lyubin, V. P., Soviet archaeologist, 40

Macrones, tribe, 74
Magdalenian culture in Georgia, 32
Maikop culture, 43–4
Maisuradze, Z., Georgian art historian, 142
Mamelukes, 113
Mamikonian, Vardan, 155
Manandyan, Acad. Ya. A., 85
Manavi castle, 124
Manazkert, battle of, 111
Manichaeans, 159
Manuel, emperor of Trebizond, 115
matriarchate, system of, 33

Medea, 64, 68, 80, 112
Media, Medes, 73–4, 83, 112
Mediterranean Sea, 39, 54, 137
megalithic structures in Georgia, 51–2
Meghvinet-ukhutsesi family, 116
Melikishvili, Prof. G. A., 59
Melkisedek, Georgian Patriarch, 134
menhirs, 52
Menua, king of Urartu, 58
Meshech, 20, 25, 56–7
Meskhians, 39, 56, 76, 82
Mesolithic period, 33–4
Mesopotamia, 39, 95, 128
Mesrop, Saint, 153
Mghvimevi, cave drawings at, 33
Michael, the Archangel, 130, 136
Michael Modrekili, 149
Midas, king, 56, 73
Miletus, 64
Mingrelia, Mingrelians, 19, 22–3, 31, 34, 59,
    75, 77, 150
Mirian, Iberian king, 91, 95, 97
Mithradates Eupator, king of Pontus, 64, 69,
    81, 99
Moaphernes, governor of Colchis, 64, 82
Mongols, 20, 177–8
Morgan, Jacques de, 29, 60
Moses of Khoni, 168–9
Moskhoi, Moskhian mountains, 50, 56, 74,
    76, 82, 89
Mossynoeci, tribe, 66–7, 74–5, 119
Motsameti, Palaeolithic remains from, 30, 33
Mousterian culture in Georgia, 31–2
Movses Daskhuranci, Armenian chronicler,
    101–2, 104
Mshvelidze, Shalva, Georgian composer, 135
Mtkvari (Kura) river, 31, 75, 80, 82, 101,
    104, 125, 155
Mtskheta, 63, 72, 82–6, 88, 91–5, 99, 101,
    103–4, 123, 128–9, 134–6, 140, 152
Muhammad the Prophet, 102
Muhammad II, Ottoman Sultan, 115
Murad-su, river, 55
Murvan Qru, Arab conqueror, 103

Mushki, tribe, 55–7, 74
Mycenae, 47–8

Nairi, 58
Nalchik cemetery, 43
Nana, Iberian queen, 91
Nemesius of Emesa, 171
Neolithic man in Georgia, 29, 34–5
New Shuamta, convent, 136
Nicaea, Council of, 94
Nicholas, Saint, 136
Nicholas II, tsar, 106
Nicopsia, 166
Nikordsminda, church at, 134
Nino, Saint, 28, 88, 91–4, 128, 134, 152, 157
Ninodsminda cathedral, 129
Ninurta, Babylonian god, 50
Nioradze, Giorgi, Georgian archaeologist,
    32–3
Nizami of Ganja, 176
Nutsubidze, Shalva, 159

Odishi, excavations at, 34–5
Odyssey, 65
Olympus, Mount, 159, 166
Omar, Caliph, 102–3
Opiza, monastery of, 141
Opizari, Beka and Beshken, goldsmiths, 141
ordeals, 118
Oshki, church, 132, 134
Ossetes, Ossetia, 20, 31, 39, 50, 60, 62, 70,
    112, 114
Ozaani, church, 148
Ozni, pottery from, 40

paganism, pagan cults in Georgia, 87–90
Palaeolithic man in Georgia, 29–33
Palestine, 22, 38, 73, 91, 98–9, 102, 111–13,
    159
Paliashvili, Zakaria, Georgian composer,
    151, 169
Panichkina, M. Z., Soviet archaeologist, 30
Paris, 142
Parnavaz, king of Georgia, 84

Parthia, 81, 86, 168
Persia, Persians, *see* Iran
Peter the Iberian, 95–6, 98, 159
Petra (Tsikhisdziri), 99–100
Petritsi, Ioane, 112, 170–2
Petritsoni monastery, Bachkovo, 159, 171
Phasis, *see* Poti; Rioni
pheasant, phasianus colchicus, 67–8
Phrixus, oracle of, 89
Phrygians, 54, 56, 73, 87
Pitiunt, *see* Bichvinta
Pitskhelauri, K. N., Georgian archaeologist, 63
Pitsunda, *see* Bichvinta
Plato, 170–2, 174
Polemo I, king of Pontus, 82
Pompey, 82, 86, 99
Pontus, 66, 74–5, 81, 99, 120
Poti (Phasis), 64, 79–80, 89–90
Prochorus the Georgian, 167
Procopius, 100
Prometheus, 60, 64, 68–71, 171
Psellos, Michael, 171
pseudo-Aristotle, 67
pseudo-Hippocrates, 81
Pshavs, Georgian mountain tribe, 64
Publicius Agrippa, 87
Pythodoris, queen of Pontus, 82

Qeenoba, carnival of, 103
Qindsvisi, church, 140
Qipchaks, 111
Qvirila, river, 128

Ras Shamra, 47
Ratcha district, 50, 75, 134
Rayy, 148
Reka, Neolithic settlement at, 34
Rgani, Palaeolithic remains from, 32
Rhea, goddess, 90
Rice, David and Tamara Talbot, 138
Rioni (Phasis) river, 23, 30–1, 59, 64–5, 67–69, 75, 81
Ripsime, Saint, 94, 129

Romanus III, Byzantine emperor, 110
Romanus IV, Byzantine emperor, 111
Rome, Romans, 81, 85–6, 99, 144
Rufinus, church history of, 91
Ruisi cathedral, 158
Ruisi-Urbnisi, synod of, 112
Runciman, Sir Steven, 106
Rusa I, king of Urartu, 56
Russia, Palaeolithic houses in, 32
Russians, 76, 96, 104, 147, 150, 178
Rustaveli, Shota, 167, 172–8
Rustavi, 144, 173

Saba, Saint, 99
Sachkhere, Bronze Age cemeteries at, 50
Sagvarjile, Palaeolithic remains from, 33
Sakartvelo, local name of Georgia, 17, 57
Sakazhia cave, 30, 33
Salmanesar III, king of Assyria, 57–8
Samara, Georgian tribal chief, 84
Samshvilde, Mousterian remains from, 31
Samtavro, 63, 72, 82, 136
Samtredia, Chalcolithic remains from, 36
Samtskhe, province, 23, 36, 39, 56, 60, 75, 89, 109, 122, 177
Samuel, Archdeacon, 154
Saqvarelidze, T., Georgian archaeologist, 40
Saracens, 102–5, 111–13
Sardaryan, S. A., Soviet archaeologist, 30
Sarduri II, king of Urartu, 59
Sargis of Tmogvi, 168
Sargon, king of Assyria, 56
Sarmatians, 20, 83, 86
Sasanids, 86, 96, 99–100, 110, 144, 154
Sasperoi, tribe, 18, 74, 76
Satani-dar, Palaeolithic remains from, 30
Schaeffer, C. F. A., 45
Scythians, 20, 63, 72–3, 76, 81–3, 86
Selene, 90
Seleucids, 83
Seljuk Turks, 20, 105, 110–11, 142, 158
Semitic languages, 23, 25
Serapion of Zarzma, Saint, 157
Serapita, princess, 152–3

Sevsamora (Tsitsamuri), 78, 82
Shamakhi, 112
Shashilu, captured by Urartians, 58
Shatberdi codex, 157
Shavsheti, province, 109, 130
Shavteli, Ioane, 167
Shengavit, excavations at, 36, 40
Shio, Saint, 140, 156
Shio-Mghwime Lavra, 139–40
Shirvan, 104, 112
Shorapani (Sarapana), 33, 50, 78, 80
Shorena, 135
Shushanik, Saint and Martyr, 97–8, 154–155
Siberia, Palaeolithic houses in, 32; pottery, 147
Sieni, king of the Daiaeni, 58
Simeon Metaphrastes, 167
Simon the Canaanite, Apostle, 166
Sinai, Mount, 109, 150, 159
Sinope, 65–6, 73, 80
Sioni basilica, 128–9
Sioni cathedral, Tbilisi, 99
Sivas, 53
Smirnov, Ya. I., 83
social structure of Iberia, 85–6
Solomon, king of Israel, 105, 158
Spain, 18, 33
Speri, *see* Ispir
Stalin, J. V., 25
Stepandsminda, 63
Stephen, Saint, 130
Stephen I, duke of Iberia, 100–1
Stephen II, duke of Iberia, 100
Steshenko-Kuftina, V., 150
Strabo, 18, 23, 64–5, 75–6, 78, 82–3, 85, 89–90, 117
Strzygowski, J., 138
Sukhumi (Dioscurias), 20, 30, 51, 64, 76, 79–81
Sultanabad, 148
Sumbat I Bagratuni, 106
Sumbat, son of David, historian, 158–9
Surami pass, 23, 77, 80

Svans, Svaneti, 19, 22–3, 53, 64, 75, 100, 123, 139
Syria, Syrians, Syriac, 22, 38–9, 73, 84, 98–99, 102, 107, 111, 128, 153–4, 156

Tabal, *see* Tubal
Tabriz, 115
Tahmasp, Shah, 126–7
Tallgren, A. M., 60
Tamar, Queen of Georgia, 28, 114–17, 150, 167, 173–4
Tao, Taokhoi, 57–9, 75–6, 82, 105, 108–10, 130–1
Taqaishvili, E. S., Georgian archaeologist, 50, 106, 128, 133
Tatian, 154
Tavadze, P., Georgian archaeologist, 40
Tavusker (Taoskari), church, 130
Tbeti monastery, 141
Tbilisi (Tiflis), 18, 36, 44, 64, 75, 83, 99–105, 109, 111, 124, 142, 144, 154, 156, 177–8
Tchqondidi, archbishop of, 116
Telavi, 167
Telipinu, Hittite deity, 53
Terek, river, 43
Terzhola district, 33
Tetramidsa, Neolithic settlement at, 34
Theodosius III, Patriarch of Antioch, 166
Thessalian houses, 37
Thierry, M. and N., 133
Tibareni, tribe, 18, 57, 66–7, 74, 76
Tiflis, *see* Tbilisi
Tiglath-pileser I, king of Assyria, 56, 58, 60
Timur Leng, 178
tin deposits in Transcaucasia, 50
Tiridates, king of Armenia, 94
Tmogvi, 128
Tolstoy, Count Leo, 161
Tornik, John, 107–8
Tortum, 132
Toumanoff, Prof. C., 95, 158
trade routes, 79–80, 104

Trebizond (Trapezus), 20, 64, 66, 75, 94, 114–15
Trialeti district, 36, 42, 44–50, 52–3, 72, 75, 88, 108–9
Troy, 50
Tsarskaya, royal graves at, 43
Tsartsis-gora, Bronze Age remains from, 50
Tsate, king of Lazica, 99
Tsebelda, inconostasis from, 139
Tsereteli, Prof. G. V., 94, 152
Tsereteli, Prof. Mikheil, 53
Tsitsishvili, Irakli, 134
Tskhinvali (Staliniri), 20, 39
Tubal, Tabal, Tubal-cain, 20, 25, 48, 50, 56–7, 66, 76
Tulepia-Melia, folk deity, 53
Turkey, Turkish, 17, 19–20, 23, 58, 85, 124, 130, 132, 178

Ubisi church, 140
Ujarma, ancient Georgian city, 123
al-'Umari, Arabic writer, 113
Uplistsikhe, ancient cave town, 82, 84–5, 125
Urartu, Urartians, 19–20, 50, 52, 54, 57–60, 69, 73–6
Urbnisi, 37, 88, 128
Urmia, lake, 58
urn burial in Georgia, 79
Utupurshini, king of the Diauehi, 58

Vakhtang Gorgaslan, king of Georgia, 98–9, 104, 134, 157
Vakhtang VI, king of Georgia, 117, 159

Vakhushti, prince of Georgia, historian and geographer, 159
Van, lake, 54, 58–9, 75
Vani, cave monastery, 177
Vardzia, cave monastery, 125–8
Varsken, Georgian apostate, 97–8, 155
Venice, 142
Vespasian, Roman emperor, 86
Vis and Ramin, romance of, 168
vishaps, sea-dragon megaliths, 52
Vitruvius, 120–2
Volga, river, 101, 156

Wardrop, Sir Oliver, 168
Wellesz, Dr Egon, 150
wergild, 117–18
Winfield, David, 132–3

Xenophon, 59, 65, 67, 74–5
Xerxes, king of Iran, 74

Yashtkhva, Palaeolithic remains from, 30
Yezdegird, king of Iran, 155

Zacharias, bishop, 157
Zakharov, A. A., 53
Zamyatnin, S. N., Soviet archaeologist, 30
Zeus, 70
Zevakh, Iberian viceroy, 85, 152
Zoroaster, Zoroastrians, 88, 90, 95, 97, 100, 152, 155
Zosime, John, Georgian scribe, 109
Zugdidi, 34
Zvartnotz, Armenian church at, 130

DATE DUE